EASY
TIKI

# EASY
# TIKI

A Modern Revival with 60 Recipes

Chloe Frechette

Photographs by Lizzie Munro
Illustrations by Spiros Halaris

PUNCH

TEN SPEED PRESS
California | New York

# CONTENTS

# DRINKS

## CLASSIC RECIPES

## MODERN RECIPES

# SYRUPS

# WELCOME TO
## EASY TIKI

Fresh on the heels of repeal, a man by the name of Donn Beach (aka Don the Beachcomber) introduced a style of drinking so flamboyant and conspicuous that it was unimaginable to a Hollywood public accustomed to the secrecy of the speakeasy. All the devices that had acted in service of discreetness during the thirteen-year "noble experiment" were flipped on their heads. Coffee cups concealing their true contents were traded for hollowed-out pineapples containing a staggering blend of rums, tropical flavors, and spices and crowned with orchids, mint, and mango leaves; the hidden entrance was replaced with a carved bamboo-and-rattan gate announcing the threshold of another world. Inside, driftwood décor, tropical plants, and the manufactured sound of rainfall signaled an exotic escape from the Depression-era reality on the other side of the entryway. It was the beginning of a movement that would come to be known as tiki.

A cursory glance at the offerings of homewares retailers and fashion labels both high and low, as well as, of course, new bars opening across the country, makes glaringly apparent one fact: we're in the midst of the second golden age of tiki. Not since its midcentury heyday has tiki's faux-island atmosphere made such a broad sweep across the country. And with tropical-themed bars opening at a rate that's hard to keep up with, tiki's momentum shows no signs of slowing.

Indeed, it's difficult to deny the appeal of the genre's aesthetic. At times when headlines seem to offer nothing but an onslaught of disheartening information, the purposefully escapist nature of the tiki bar—no TVs, no windows—is an apt antidote. But for a category whose appeal hinges on the impression of "the easy life," tiki drinks are among the hardest to make, often calling for upward of ten ingredients and a host of specialized techniques and tools, not to mention elaborate, over-the-top garnishes. The Zombie, for example, calls for between nine and eleven ingredients (depending on whether you make the 1934 version or the 1956 version), while the QB Cooler calls for ten, and the Kikuya Lapu for twelve.

Of course, it takes more than a laundry list of ingredients or tropical flavors to label a drink "tiki." Decidedly untropical cocktails can climb toward ten ingredients without qualifying, while the Mai Tai, perhaps tiki's most iconic output, clocks in at a mere five. The transportive power of its simple construction hints at a more abstract set of criteria required to earn the "tiki" label, beyond the "more is more" approach that characterizes much of the category. Chief among them is the ability for a cocktail to conjure another world through its composition, presentation, and name. Missionary's Downfall and Cobra's Fang, for example, are far more evocative than pineapple sour and tropical rum punch.

As you'll see throughout this book, it's possible to expand the tiki template with drinks designed to match the ease of the tiki lifestyle— without losing its quintessential character. In fact, Donn Beach, the founding father of tiki itself, set a precedent for such a practice with simplified versions of his Zombie and Planter's Punch designed for home bartenders. But today, the advent of new ingredients and techniques, from fat-washing to acid-adjusting citrus, has only further complicated the genre. Within these pages, however, is a new set of simplified drinks designed for the revival age, which aim to bring tiki back within the home bartender's reach.

## How to Use This Book

So much of tiki's identity hinges on the appearance of extravagance. The very foundation of the genre is, after all, the willful complication of a simple punch recipe. But difficulty is by no means a prerequisite, and the aim of this book is to offer an approach to making tiki cocktails that feels accessible but not dumbed down.

"There's no definition in the dictionary that says tiki has to be complicated," says Jeff "Beachbum" Berry, tiki author, historian, and bar owner. "There are so many arbitrary things that people say define tiki: it has to have crushed ice in it, and it has to have twelve ingredients. . . . Does it really?"

When Berry opened Latitude 29 in 2014 in New Orleans's French Quarter, it opened his eyes to the importance of simplification. Prior to owning his own bar, his objective had largely been to rescue extinct recipes and re-create them in their truest historic form even if it meant dipping into an $80 bottle of rum for a drink that took half an hour to build. Now there are other considerations to keep in mind. "There are three layers," he explains. "The first layer is always 'How do I make the best possible drink?' The next layer is 'in the least amount of time.' And the third layer is 'for the least amount of money'—because you've got to stay in business."

To this end, Berry takes the famous Don the Beachcomber ethos "What one rum can't do, three rums can" and flips it on its head, seeking out exceptional bottles of rum that can do the work of three. To maximize returns on the least amount of effort, the same considerations went into sourcing the recipes for *Easy Tiki*.

Across the sixty cocktail recipes within these pages—twenty classic and forty modern—ingredients clock in at six or fewer. What's more, house-made syrups are kept to a minimum and are standardized across the board (so there's no need to make one version of cinnamon syrup for one recipe and another version for the next), and most require little to no cooking. For the recipes that reinterpret classics that originally comprised more than six ingredients, I worked with top bartenders to capture the drinks' essence in a home-bartender-friendly manner.

Of course, information on the best rums to use in each drink, how to build a home tiki bar, and tips for styling each cocktail with appropriately tropical flair can be found in the following pages, too, alongside the ever-important skill of batching for a crowd. And for those newly acquainted with tiki or simply looking for a refresher on how the style came to be, there's a chapter dedicated to precisely that, followed by a snapshot of where the category stands today and the best places to tiki from coast to coast, including historic bastions of the style and modern trailblazers.

# WHAT IS TIKI?

# When the first-ever Pearl Diver Punch emerged from a discreet bar

at Los Angeles's Don the Beachcomber in the 1930s, it signaled a dramatic shift. The drink, festooned with a geranium leaf and edible flowers and served in a bespoke glass, was the antithesis of the spartan three-ingredient formulas—the Manhattan, Martini, Old-Fashioned—that had defined the bar world's status quo for the last half century. It belonged to an entirely new category of cocktail. Today we call it tiki, but it wasn't always so.

"Back in the day, during the golden age of what we now call tiki drinks, they were never called that," explains Jeff "Beachbum" Berry. "It's a retro term coined by cocktail renaissance writers and bloggers and cocktail categorizers to provide some kind of nomenclature for the style of drink." During their midcentury heyday, "tiki drinks" were known interchangeably as exotic cocktails, tropical cocktails, Polynesian drinks, or, in Don the Beachcomber's parlance, "rhum rhapsodies." (Only after the drinks had faded from mainstream phenomenon to cultural artifact did the name emerge, borrowing from the central motif of what historian Sven Kirsten labels the "high tiki style" tiki totems.)

It was, in part, the very drama of these eye-catching drinks—the Shark's Tooth, Missionary's Downfall, the Zombie—that allowed the genre to evade codification for so long. The formulas themselves, with their complex blends of rums and unusual modifiers such as falernum and orgeat, were ruled by a certain behind-the-scenes rigorousness. But from the outside, the imprecise notion that "you know it when you see it" has long dictated the limits (or lack thereof) of tiki. "When you start calling something a tiki drink, now you have to define that," says Berry. But nobody did.

Of course, there's a reason—beyond the human need to label, sort, and categorize—that enthusiasts and experts alike squabble over the meaning and parameters of tiki; it's the same reason that the volume of titles dedicated to the topic grows larger by the day and new bars devoted to its legacy are on the rise. There's something singular about tiki drinks—something that gets lost when they're thrown under the umbrella category "tropical."

So what is a tiki drink?

"It all comes down to the punch formula," says Berry, referencing the classic Planter's Punch cocktail, a West Indies staple since the colonial era. The components of the cocktail are immortalized in an oft trotted-out rhyme: one of sour, two of sweet, three of strong, and four of weak—referring to citrus, sweetener, spirit, and dilution (in the form of water, ice, or tea), respectively. What tiki does is fracture each of these requisite components so there are multiples of each. Or, as Berry summarizes, "It's a Caribbean drink squared, or cubed."

Where a typical punch recipe might call for lime as the sole sour element, tiki will call for lime and grapefruit, or even lime, grapefruit, and passion fruit. For the sweet element, in place of just simple syrup, honey or maple syrup might also make an appearance. But perhaps most significant is the amplification of the "strong" component. Never before had a mixed drink doubled down on the base spirit by splitting it into multiple rums, or even multiple spirits, like rum and brandy in the Scorpion, but doing so would become a hallmark of the style.

"It's a baroque Planter's Punch," echoes Martin Cate, owner of San Francisco tiki mecca Smuggler's Cove. But for Cate, what separates a tiki drink from tropical drinks, its closest relatives, beyond its amplified construction, is the added element of spice. "Tiki has a clear definition of what it's supposed to be," he says. "It has to have sour, sweet, spirit working in equal and interesting ways, complex ways, and it has to have—in my take—some kind of spice component to it. The spice really takes it to the next level."

Indeed, spice is a key component of many tiki recipes, particularly those drawn from Don the Beachcomber's library of work, and it can come into play in many forms, from syrups to bitters to freshly grated nutmeg. But does the identity of the entire tiki style rest on such a minute detail as a dusting of nutmeg or cinnamon? Is that all that stands between tiki and tropical?

Yes and no. But a more concrete answer begins with explaining why, for instance, a Piña Colada is categorically not a tiki drink. With its pineapple wedge and umbrella it certainly looks the part. At its core, however, its rum-pineapple-coconut construction lacks the requisite sour element of a Planter's Punch (and, in fact, many Caribbean classics such as the Daiquiri and the Mojito). Created in the 1950s at a resort in San Juan, Puerto Rico, the Piña Colada slots better into a category known as "resort drinks" or "boat drinks," which, by the 1970s, had subsumed the title "tropical."

"They don't have the balance. They don't have the structure. They don't have the structural integrity of tiki," says Cate of these devolved tropical drinks. Berry expresses a similar sentiment. "Boat drinks were kind of a mutation of both tiki and pre-Prohibition tropical drinks," he says, citing the Piña Colada as a prime example. "It's sweet and strong; there's no sour."

That tiki and tropical would become conflated, particularly in the 1970s, however, is not all that surprising. The era saw the rise of sour mix and juices from concentrate, and tiki was not immune. Even at historic tiki temples, canned fruit and fruit juice became the norm, not the exception. In such a landscape, the balance, complexity, and depth that made tiki unique were certainly harder to strike, and the line between tiki and tropical melted.

The conflation of the two terms seemed to diminish another key point of differentiation between tropical and tiki, namely that the latter sparked a robust culture that went well beyond a genre of cocktails to span décor, architecture, sculpture, glassware, cuisine, and apparel. Tiki was, in other words, an all-encompassing lifestyle.

Entire industries emerged and artists' careers thrived around the need to feed the hunger for faux Polynesian art and design in the early twentieth century. Nowhere was this truer than in Hawaii. The imagined home-land of the movement, the tropical islands of Hawaii were, in fact, late adopters of tiki, with much of the requisite décor supplied by mainland

# YOU KNOW IT
## WHEN YOU SEE IT

More important than ticking particular boxes flavor-wise is the overall intention of a tiki drink. The combination of the characteristics that follow are good indicators that the drink in question possesses the ability to transport you out of the humdrum, the ordinary, the mundane.

## The Name Says It All

Shark's Tooth, Cobra's Fang, the Vicious Virgin. Without even knowing the contents of each of these cocktails, it's clear that they offer something different than a tropical punch—even if they're composed of the same ingredients. The name provides the first bit of intrigue and mystery and, in the mind of the drinker, sets the stage for what's to come.

## Complexity Is Key

Part of what separates tiki from the broader family of tropical and Caribbean drinks is a layered complexity that comes courtesy of multiples— multiple sours, multiple sweetnesses, multiple spirits. But complexity is not synonymous with a specific number of ingredients. Even in cases where the drink does not follow the rules of multiples, like the Mai Tai, it should still demonstrate balance between those essential components of the original Planter's Punch. Often, but not always, spice will play into the formula, too.

## Drama Club

From the glass fishing bobs to the thatched roof to the flaming lime hulls tossed atop heaps of crushed ice, theatricality is the raison d'être of tiki. When it comes to the drink itself, glassware and garnish play a big part. Tiki gave rise to a number of unique glasses, like the ribbed Pearl Diver glass and, of course, the countless custom tiki mugs unique to each bar across the country. Often opaque, these carved mugs play into the mystery of the genre, obscuring the cocktail within, while elaborate garnishes of edible flowers and bananas carved to look like dolphins or other sea creatures enhance the sense of drama.

artists. A man by the name of Edward Brownlee, who happened upon a book of Oceanic art at the California College of Arts and Crafts, quickly became the de facto tiki carver and the arbiter of the tiki aesthetic when Donn employed him to execute all of Waikiki's International Market Place, a sprawling complex that would go on to house three of Donn Beach's own bars. Brownlee's work was a prime example of the nature of tiki. At one point the difference between a tropical drink and a tiki drink was defined by where it was served.

Today, however, just as tropical and tiki were uniformly dismissed at the end of the twentieth century, the two are once again intertwined, this time under the umbrella of "craft cocktails." The same forces that rescued the stalwarts of the golden age of cocktails, such as the Manhattan and the Sazerac, as well as the oft-derided 1990s-era drinks like the Cosmopolitan and the Amaretto Sour, salvaged their tropical brethren. The philosophy that "no drink was beyond rescuing if executed with thoughtful ingredients and proper technique" elevated boat drinks from insipid concoctions lacking balance and complexity to dignified cocktail-bar fare, returning tiki to its rightful station as one of the most nuanced cocktail categories.

When a balanced Piña Colada that consists of more than just canned juice and rum can be had under the same roof as a proper Zombie, the conflation of tropical and tiki is far less egregious. Hardliners will stick to their guns, requiring at least some element of spice, but such a stance overlooks an essential shared characteristic between tiki and tropical: both possess the ability to transport the drinker to far-flung places through the evocative flavors inside the glass. More so than traditional cocktails, tiki and tropical enlist all the senses in the name of escapism. Before experiencing the twists and turns of their multilayered compositions, your eye is first met with a feast of its own: an ice cave, a hollowed-out coconut, or an intricate decorative mug containing the mysterious drink. Further obscuring the contents of the glass is a cornucopia of edible flowers, tropical fruit, and aromatic herbs and bitters. All this ensures that every sense is taken on the same journey. To try to cordon off tiki from tropical proves a fruitless detour down the path of semantics. As Berry observes, "You're creating parameters that never were, for a category that never was." Better just to take a sip and dive in.

# CREATING THE
## TIKI ATMOSPHERE

Tiki is more than just cocktails. Historically, tiki culture has enveloped a broad swath of creative endeavors, from architecture to fine art to music. This transportive atmosphere is central to the genre. Just as the golden age of tiki had its share of mainstream artists and musicians whose work infiltrated the popular tiki bars of the mid-twentieth century, not to mention home tiki bars, today's revival boasts a cohort of dedicated artists and musicians whose work can help transform your own tiki experience.

## Art and Décor

Pineapple-shaped drinking vessels can now be found at mainstream retailers, and it's no longer uncommon for tiki-inspired design elements, like tropical wallpaper, to creep into non-tiki bars. But there are a number of artists producing contemporary works of art that pay homage to both the style and subjects of tiki's midcentury moment. One such artist is Josh Agle, who goes by the nickname Shag. A painter, illustrator, and tiki-mug ceramicist, his works can be found at the Shag Store in Palm Springs. Other fixtures in the tiki art community include "Crazy Al" Evans, Bamboo Ben, Bosco, and Gecko.

## Music

In 1957, Martin Denny released an album called *Exotica*. It was a record so influential that it would go on to lend its name to an entire genre of music defined by its pseudo-Oceanic sound, courtesy of bongos, gongs, and bird calls. Denny described the sound as "a combination of the South Pacific and the Orient . . . what a lot of people imagined the islands to be like. . . . It's pure fantasy, though." There could be no more apt a soundtrack to tiki. It was a style also practiced by the likes of Les Baxter, Tak Shindo, and Arthur Lyman, all of whom were household names during the golden age of tiki.

Just as tiki is experiencing a revival on the cocktail front, exotica music is likewise seeing an uptick in both practitioners and enthusiasts. In 2014, Alika Lyman paid tribute to his great-uncle Arthur Lyman with two volumes of lounge music called *Leis of Jazz*, while the groups Kava Kon, Clouseaux, and Mr. Ho's Orchestratica are also popular.

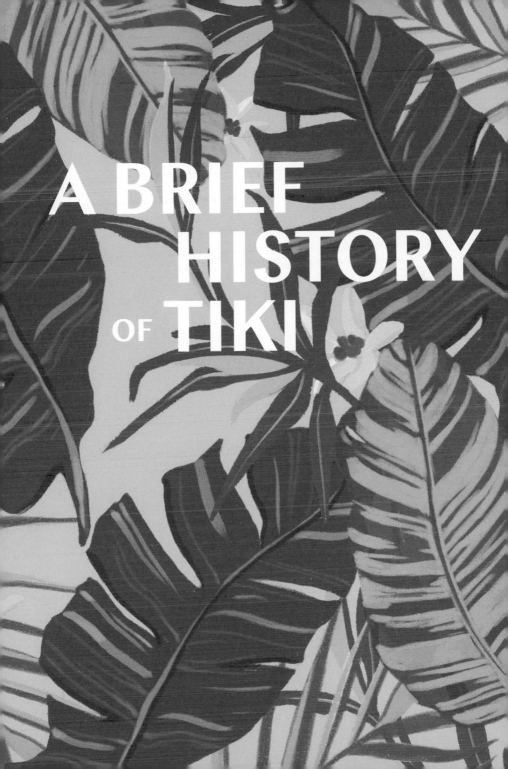

# A BRIEF
# HISTORY
## OF TIKI

# For nearly half a century, from the 1930s through the 1970s, tiki fever swept the nation.

And unlike so much in the murky depths of cocktail history, it's possible to pinpoint the precise moment that changed everything. The ember that sparked the tiki blaze was one precocious twenty-seven-year-old, who, in 1934, opened the world's first tiki bar.

Ernest Raymond Beaumont Gantt was born in 1907 in Jamaica—at least according to his own account. Records discovered in 2015 by historian David Wondrich, however, reveal that Gantt was actually born in Mexia, Texas, a fact with which he was not forthcoming. A man of mystery from the start, Gantt fabricated a "beachcomber" persona for himself, the depth and detail of which mirrored the elaborate nature of the culture he would single-handedly usher into existence with the debut of Don's Beachcomber Café and the "rhum rhapsodies" served within.

When he was eighteen years old, Gantt set off on a world tour spanning the Caribbean, South Pacific, and beyond, returning to U.S. soil with a bounty of carvings, ornaments, and assorted flotsam in tow. In 1933, he secured a permanent home in which to hang his hat and his accumulated miscellany: a nondescript one-room space on North McCadden Place in Los Angeles. There, he erected a rudimentary bamboo-and-rattan gate, above which he fastened a driftwood sign bearing what would become the most famous name in Hollywood: Don's Beachcomber. Inside, he built a twenty-four-seat bamboo-fronted bar with Japanese fishing floats, a thatched ceiling, tropical plants, and bundles of bananas strewn behind the bar. During service, elaborate drinks garnished in a rococo fashion would emerge from behind a screen, where they were prepared by a group of Filipino bartenders known as the Four Boys.

This was in part a ploy to build intrigue, but at the same time, it served to protect the secrets of Gantt's recipes, which he kept close to his chest at all times. Even his trusty team of bartenders, who worked entirely out of the view of the public eye, knew the recipes only by their given codes. As a precaution against theft of his intellectual property, Gantt would premix his syrups, spices, and rum blends and assign them each a number and the moniker "Donn's Spices" or "Donn's Mix"—their precise composition known to no one but himself.

It wasn't just paranoia that motivated this strategy. As enviable as the drinks were in appearance, for competing bar owners, the secrets of their construction were even more desirable. Just as Gantt melded cultures together in the look and feel of his bar, his original drinks fused Caribbean and California influence, creating an entirely new style, the first to emerge since the golden age of cocktails decades earlier. Never before had different styles of rum from various countries of origin been blended within a single cocktail, and Gantt's penchant for pulling from the abundance of produce readily available to him in Southern California gave his drinks an unparalleled brightness. The notion of splitting the base spirit to achieve a more nuanced profile was wholly novel and became a signature of Gantt's style, along with the addition of spice, which he included in the form of syrups or bitters and as a garnish grated over a drink.

Don's Beachcomber Café was, according to Martin Cate in *Smuggler's Cove*, the first bar to "match over-the-top drinks to the over-the-top décor." The novel bar quickly captured Hollywood's attention, and by 1937, due to its growing popularity, Gantt was forced to move his operation to a neighboring property, where he rechristened the bar Don the Beachcomber, an homage to the name he had gone by during his time as a Prohibition-era rumrunner. Not long after, Gantt would change his legal name, too, to Donn Beach, and today he is often referred to as either Donn Beach or Don the Beachcomber.

Typically adorned in white shorts, a white button-down shirt, and a Havana hat, Donn's signature beachcomber style caught more than just the attention of Hollywood's elite. And it didn't take long for imitators to crop up, seeking to replicate the success of the Hollywood hotshot and his namesake bar.

Chief among them was Vic Bergeron. The very year that Donn Beach opened his expanded bar, Bergeron, then the owner of a small Oakland restaurant by the name of Hinky Dinks, paid his first visit. The trip would prove to be hugely influential on his own business—a fact that Bergeron never denied. Upon returning home, he and his wife quickly transformed Hinky Dinks into their own tropical oasis, festooned with decorative curios culled from friends and acquaintances (including Donn Beach), often in exchange for meals and drinks, earning him the nickname Trader Vic.

But Vic was more than merely an imitator, and he brought his own aesthetic to his establishments and the drinks he served. Soon he was the bartender whom other bartenders sought to replicate—an easier feat, considering Trader Vic published nine volumes of recipe books in his lifetime to Donn's zero.

From a design perspective, his aesthetic skewed slightly more industrial; ropes and nautical touches, like anchors, barrels, and lanterns, were the norm. As for his cocktails, he introduced a score of ingredients that had never been seen in tropical mixed drinks before, including orgeat, an almond syrup he encountered in his mother's cooking, and okolehao, a native Hawaiian distillate. Where Donn was known for his rum blends, Vic became known for combining different spirits together. His Fog Cutter, for example, marries gin, rum, and cognac, with a sherry float in a heady mixture that lives up to its name.

In his lifetime, Vic would open two dozen Trader Vic's locations across the globe, from Scottsdale to Vancouver to London. The franchise lives on today, with nearly twenty existing locations, several of which were established during Vic's lifetime. Donn, too, started an empire, with outposts of his Beachcomber Café opening in Palm Springs, Chicago, and beyond. The expansion was largely thanks to his entrepreneurial wife, Sunny Sund, to whom Donn ceded control of the franchise and who grew the business sixteenfold while Donn was deployed overseas during World War II. The only problem was, when the couple divorced in 1940, their agreement stipulated that Donn could not open another location within the United States. In 1945, Donn headed to Hawaii, the spiritual homeland of tiki—and a place beyond the reach of the divorce decree, which only extended to the *mainland* United States—to open a Don the Beachcomber in Waikiki.

While Donn was bringing faux Polynesian drinks to Polynesia, back on the mainland, his acolytes were busy feeding the tiki craze. One of Donn's key bartenders, Ray Buhen, part of the famed Four Boys, traded his allegiance to the Seven Seas, a rival establishment that opened on Hollywood Boulevard in 1937, then he spent time behind the bar at Sugie Tropics on Rodeo Drive. After actor-turned-restaurateur Steve Crane purchased Sugie Tropics and converted it into the famous Luau, Buhen graduated to bartending front of house, and in 1961, went on to open Tiki-Ti on Sunset Boulevard, a golden age hotspot that still stands today. Even as the Beachcomber staff scattered—lured by higher wages from competitive bar owners—Donn's recipes remained a mystery, their code unbreakable. But that did little to stymie the swell of tiki bars that cropped up in the wake of the Beachcomber's success.

Bars and restaurants such as the Kon-Tiki (named for the Academy Award–winning documentary of the same name, chronicling one man's journey from Peru to Polynesia on a wooden raft), the Luau, and the Kona Kai capitalized not only on the original Beachcomber's success but on a wider cultural fascination with Polynesia that gripped the nation in the 1950s and '60s. With thousands of veterans returning from the South Pacific warfront, there was a growing interest in the climate, culture, and aesthetic of that corner of the world—whether real or imagined—which fed the homegrown tiki trend. Following the success of Don's Beachcomber Café and Don the Beachcomber, thousands of Polynesian-inspired restaurants and bars opened their doors in the successive decades.

Not long after tiki reached its peak in the 1960s, changing tastes ushered in its demise. The 1970s heralded an era when fresh ingredients were increasingly eschewed. Drinks such as the Piña Colada and Sex on the Beach gained traction, displacing the nuance of their tiki predecessors and giving rise to the era of so-called boat drinks. It would take the arrival of the craft cocktail renaissance in the early 2000s to rescue both tropical and tiki from the trash bin of history.

# THE TWO
## SCHOOLS OF TIKI

It would not be an exaggeration to say that every so-called tiki cocktail served during the golden age of tiki—and indeed today's modern tiki revival—was owed, in no small part, to the imagination of Donn Beach and his greatest imitator, Trader Vic. You'd be hard-pressed to find a recipe that can't be traced back to the foundational building blocks of Donn's rhum rhapsodies. Without his singular vision for a faux-tropical oasis off Hollywood Boulevard, and Vic's additions to the tiki canon and subsequent tiki empire, there would be little for today's revival to draw upon.

## Don the Beachcomber

The founding father of the tiki movement, Donn Beach's recipes became widely imitated almost from the second he opened the doors to his North McCadden Place institution, despite the secrecy surrounding them. For years, Jeff "Beachbum" Berry has been working to crack the code of those original recipes, publishing his findings in a series of books, most notably *Sippin' Safari*, first released in 2007. His work has helped shed light on the characteristics of Don the Beachcomber's signature palette.

### Rum, Spice, and Everything Nice

Though hardly cutting edge by today's standards, in which it's not uncommon for an Old-Fashioned or a Martini to feature a split base of whiskey or gin, Don the Beachcomber's layered rhum rhapsodies were entirely groundbreaking when he began serving them in the early 1930s. Mixing dark and light rums, not to mention rums from different countries of origin, had never been done before. It brought a depth to his creations that was further enhanced by adding a fifth component to the four in the original Planter's Punch formula: spice. Ingredients such as ginger, nutmeg, allspice, and cinnamon, often incorporated through spiced syrups or liqueurs, added new dimensions to his explosive punches and became central to his personal profile.

### The Original Farm-to-Glass

Donn Beach relied heavily on the abundance of citrus that was readily available to him in the climes of Southern California. Fresh limes, grapefruit, and oranges were deployed alongside fresh mint and honey to provide a three-dimensional brightness to his drinks. Eschewing ingredients that did not grow in his geographic region lent his creations an early farm-to-glass bent.

## Trader Vic

Having done his best to reverse engineer the drinks served by Don the Beachcomber, Trader Vic hit upon his own style, sharing certain characteristics with his original competition but ultimately finding ingredients and flavor combinations that were entirely his own.

### Rum and Then Some

Trader Vic similarly layered rums in the style of Don the Beachcomber, but he took the practice a step further, marrying an array of spirits within a single drink. His Fog Cutter is perhaps the best example, combining rum, gin, and cognac with lemon juice, orange juice, and orgeat and topping the whole mixture with a float of sherry.

### More Is More

Trader Vic introduced a number of ingredients that had previously never appeared in the tropical-cocktail realm. Apart from the sherry, gin, and cognac in his Fog Cutter, he experimented with sweet vermouth, maraschino, Scotch, and a number of other spirits and liqueurs, including okolehao, a type of Hawaiian moonshine. On the nonalcoholic side, he leaned on lemon, something Don the Beachcomber never favored, and banana—a key component in his Banana Cow, one of the earliest tiki-inspired recipes he created and served at Hinky Dink's before converting the bar into the full-on tropical oasis of Trader Vic's. Arguably, his most significant addition to the tiki palette was orgeat, an almond syrup that appears in many of his recipes.

# THE MODERN
# TIKI REVIVAL

# Forty years ago, tiki was as good as dead, a victim of shifting tastes.

The earnest escapism of the tiki era was traded for a different sort of glamour in the 1970s and '80s, an aesthetic once defined by disco drinks and Cosmopolitans. The vintage décor and tiki mugs that today might fetch hundreds of dollars on eBay—if you can find them at all—were relegated to thrift stores and garage sales, the discarded bric-a-brac of a forgotten era. On North McCadden Place in Los Angeles, ground zero for the entire tiki phenomenon, not so much as a plaque could be seen to commemorate the site of Don the Beachcomber.

That we even know the locations of these bygone tiki temples, their names, who frequented them, and what was served in each is entirely thanks to a small group of highly dedicated individuals, whose passion, determination, and collaborative spirit helped set in motion a series of events that collectively rescued tiki from the brink of extinction.

When these so-called tiki revivalists began their work, there wasn't the possibility to crowdsource answers, because, well, there was no crowd. "It was a very small world of people talking," remembers Martin Cate of those early years. Many of the conversations that would become watershed moments in tiki's resurgence happened face to face. In the pre-internet days of the 1980s and '90s, that such connections could be made at all was the product of equal parts dedication and destiny. "There really was some kind of kismet involved," says Jeff "Beachbum" Berry, the most central figure in tiki's modern revival.

To describe the encounters that led to tiki's current revival would require another book, but the following are the central players and pivotal moments responsible for the second golden age that we're enjoying today.

# Sven Kirsten—The Historian

A cinematographer by trade and an archeologist at heart, Sven Kirsten's interests lay in discovering and documenting the remnants of a culture swiftly fading from collective memory.

His interest in the category was first piqued when he encountered a number of vintage tiki menus at Los Angeles's Oceanic Arts, a store dedicated to tropical décor, in 1989. He was immediately taken by the graphic design displayed on their pages. His fascination with these menus, which he describes as "oil paintings of tiki style," sparked a greater attention to the iconography of tiki as a whole.

Not long after, he set about exploring the Los Angeles area in search of any remnant he could find of what he would come to term "Polynesian Pop"—a catchall name for the material culture of tiki, which extended to everything from matchbooks to apartment complexes drawing on the faux-Polynesian style. His pursuit took him zigzagging across the country, a journey that would ultimately provide the source material for *The Book of Tiki*, his 2003 volume documenting and analyzing the craze of Polynesian Pop that swept the country in the 1950s. Thanks to his efforts, we have a printed record of tiki locations across the nation, many of which would have otherwise been lost to the world.

Beyond this, however, Kirsten provided a framework within which to chart the trajectory of the tiki movement. From his rich database of ephemera, photographs, and objects, he was able to break down the tiki output into four main aesthetic eras known today as Pre-Tiki, Beachcomber Style, Trader Style, and Tiki (or High Tiki), each corresponding to a particular phase in tiki's greater evolution. Such a classification system offered a lens to better understand the complete picture of what had been lost and what was actively being razed and forgotten.

Through a series of lectures that he organized at the Los Angeles Forum for Architecture and Urban Design, Kirsten shared his findings with a growing group of like-minded individuals, including a graphic artist named Otto von Stroheim.

## Otto von Stroheim—The Organizer

Without Otto von Stroheim, tiki revivalists might never have banded together as they did. He was, in many ways, the hub around which the movement grew, responsible for bringing people together through a series of organized events and his zine, *Tiki News*, which covered the history and current state of tiki, the first publication dedicated exclusively to the topic.

Like Kirsten, von Stroheim's entry point into tiki was not through the drinks themselves but rather through the lounge music played where these drinks were served. It didn't take long, however, for his interest to expand to encompass all things tiki. By the mid-1990s, he had become a collector and avid preservationist of tiki culture. In fact, the very first issue of *Tiki News*, in January 1995, set out the following decrees: "It is our mission to preserve any and all remaining elements from the Polynesian Pop era" and "We intend to create a forum for sharing current and past information regarding any sort of tiki culture."

It was through *Tiki News* that Jennifer Santiago, the daughter of original Don the Beachcomber maître d' Dick Santiago, was introduced to Jeff "Beachbum" Berry, setting in motion one of the most significant discoveries in recent tiki history (more on that later). The audience of *Tiki News* also made apparent that there was enough of a following to coordinate an event series, drawing readers together for in-person meet-ups. The first formal event von Stroheim coordinated, called Planet Tiki: Bongos by the Bay, took place in San Francisco in 1999. In 2001, he launched a more ambitious event under the name Tiki Oasis, which continues into the present, consisting of several days of seminars, parties, and, of course, copious cocktails.

# Jeff "Beachbum" Berry—The Codebreaker

In modern tiki, all roads lead back to Jeff "Beachbum" Berry. Without him, our cocktail lexicons would be deprived of the Zombie, the Pearl Diver, the Nui Nui, and countless other historic tropical recipes. His singular determination to crack Don the Beachcomber's cryptic recipes—a task that took more than a decade—unlocked an invaluable chapter in drinks history, one that enriched our understanding of tiki as a whole.

Unlike his more prolific successor, Trader Vic, Don the Beachcomber never published his recipes, viewing them as valuable trade secrets to be protected at all costs—indecipherable even by his own staff. To re-create any of the Beachcomber's work would require first tracking down the formulas, cracking their code, and finding the called-for ingredients, many of which had been discontinued.

Berry, one of the few tiki revivalists to pay particular interest to the drinks being served within these exotic cocktail bars ("most were interested in the lifestyle stuff," he says), began his search by tracking down members of the Don the Beachcomber diaspora in his hometown of Los Angeles, hoping they might part with what knowledge they had of the recipes they used to serve. "Nobody would tell me anything," remembers Berry, noting either a prolonged loyalty or a genuine lack of information.

His lucky break came in 2005, when—connected through von Stroheim's *Tiki News*—Jennifer Santiago, daughter of Dick Santiago, an original Don the Beachcomber maître d', offered him her late father's notebook, which contained a number of handwritten recipes from Dick's years at the original establishment. But it was no Rosetta stone; it would take two years from the time Berry received the recipes for him to decode them.

While certain ingredients were decidedly straightforward—Jamaican rum, Puerto Rican rum—others required additional research. "It said 'three-quarters ounce mix,'" remembers Berry of one particular recipe. This was one of several undisclosed proprietary mixes and spices called for in the pages of Santiago's notebook that would only reveal themselves through a series of chance encounters with veteran tiki bartenders over the course of several years.

Even in the cases where the ingredients were entirely decipherable, Berry often encountered products that were no longer commercially produced. To overcome this hurdle, he teamed up with the only other person he knew at the time who had an interest in vintage cocktails: Ted Haigh, a graphic designer in the film industry. Introduced by Sven Kirsten (the two had worked on a film together, by chance), Ted Haigh "was like a complete character," says Berry. "He was like a charming visitor from the 1920s. He drove an old Duesenberg and dressed in vintage clothing and hats, and he was really into vintage cocktails," remembers Berry. "I had never met anybody who was into vintage cocktails. It was like meeting a cult of one."

Together, Berry and Haigh trawled Southern California for their respective holy grails. For Haigh, who would go on to author *Vintage Spirits and Forgotten Cocktails*, it was extinct liqueurs, like crème de violette and cordial-médoc; for Berry, it was falernum (a spiced Caribbean cordial) and Demerara rum. "We would get into his vintage convertible and drive up and down San Bernardino and Pasadena looking for the crappiest old broken-down liquor stores you could find," remembers Berry. "That's how we found a lot of stuff."

On one particular trip to a liquor store in Beverly Hills, the two happened upon a treasure trove of old falernum. Knowing they might not chance upon another bottle of the stuff, Haigh called up the proprietor of Fee Brothers, a fourth-generation cocktail bitters and syrups producer, who agreed to reverse engineer it. "That's how we could make those drinks in the late nineties, early aughts," says Berry.

It took a team of three people to resurrect just one lost ingredient, but Berry didn't stop there. He would go on to find the nearest approximations for bygone rums, often with the help of Stephen Remsberg, owner of the largest private collection of vintage rum in the United States. Together with his wife, Annene Kaye—a former bartender herself—Berry pieced together historic recipes that would have otherwise died out entirely. He penned the results in what would become the tiki revival's essential reading: *Beachbum Berry's Grog Log* and *Beachbum Berry's Intoxica* and, later, *Sippin' Safari*; without which, today's tiki bars would only be guessing at the contents of many of their drinks.

## Martin Cate—The Bar Builder

When Martin Cate opened Forbidden Island in Alameda, California, in 2006, he put Berry's rediscovered recipes into action, becoming the first tiki bar to apply a craft cocktail sensibility, which had been establishing itself over the past decade. In calling on fresh juices, house-made syrups, and a thoughtful approach to drink-making, Cate elevated tiki back to its former glory and, crucially, animated what were simply words on a page into a living, breathing entity. As Cate describes it, "Jeff sort of drew the battle plans, and I went to the front line by opening my places."

In 2009, Cate opened Smuggler's Cove in San Francisco, where he took the concept even further—procuring vintage Trader Vic memorabilia and commissioning bespoke water features and custom pieces from contemporary tiki artists, all in service to an immersive forty-nine-seat tiki experience. Cate's commitment to creating an entire world discrete from the reality outside its doors was thoroughly in line with the tiki bars of the golden age. But its reliance on a network of contemporary tikiphiles—artists, bartenders, designers—signaled a new dawn for the genre, paving a way for its continued evolution.

Beyond Smuggler's Cove, however, Cate has had a hand in the development of a number of the most notable tiki bars of the modern age, including False Idol in San Diego, Hale Pale in Portland, and, most recently, Max's South Seas Hideaway in Grand Rapids, Michigan. The latter is undoubtedly his grandest undertaking yet, with three stories dedicated to authentic midcentury artifacts and custom pieces from renowned tiki artist Gecko. At each property, Cate continues to demonstrate his commitment to the immersive aesthetic of tiki and his penchant for manufacturing escapism on a grand scale.

## The Modern Torchbearers

Just as Cate himself applied the techniques of the craft cocktail renaissance to tiki, bringing it up to date in the early 2000s, the next generation of tiki bartenders is not only keeping the tiki torch lit but pushing the boundaries of the genre to keep in step with larger cocktail trends.

In 2015, Paul McGee and Shelby Allison opened Lost Lake in Chicago, a city with a long affinity for tropical-minded cocktails. It's a bar that feels undeniably linked to the great tiki temples of the past, without feeling outdated. Extravagance—in elaborate garnishes and presentation—is balanced by responsible waste management, while heavy-hitting rum cocktails share menu pages with low-proof and no-proof tropical drinks.

Garret Richard likewise brings a twenty-first-century sensibility to his take on tiki. In his interpretations of classic tiki cocktails, which he serves alongside original creations at his Exotica pop-up series, Richard strives to bring every component back in line with how it would've tasted at the time of its creation, using of-the-moment techniques. Noting that grapefruits were more acidic in the past than they are now, he'll often acid-adjust his citrus or explore new infusion techniques to achieve the desired flavor profile.

Perhaps more than any other modern practitioner of tiki, Brian Miller's drinks reflect a modern crossover of tiki techniques applied to non-tiki ingredients. Take his Double Barrel Winchester, for example. In this gin-based riff on the Zombie, Miller uses four different gins, which he layers much the same way Don the Beachcomber layered rums to achieve an effect not replicable by any single bottle. It's an approach that represents the inveroc of a larger trend that sees tiki's core flavor palette—falernum, orgeat, allspice—making its way into drinks served outside tiki bars. That these crossover drinks have such widespread appeal is a testament to the strength and staying power of tiki.

Not since the golden age of tiki has there been more interest in the creations of Don the Beachcomber, Trader Vic, and their many imitators. It's a phenomenon whose impact can be felt even by the few holdovers from the first tiki era, like the Mai-Kai and the Tiki-Ti, which have become destinations for a new generation of tikiphiles and continue to evolve into twenty-first-century iterations of their former selves.

Like any great fantasy universe, from *Star Wars* to Marvel, the only limit on the evolution of tiki today is that of our own imagination.

# EASY TIKI
## COCKTAILS
### (IN SIX INGREDIENTS OR FEWER)

# The time it takes to craft a delicious cocktail should not exceed the time it takes to enjoy it.

To this end, these recipes aim to minimize futzing as much as possible. The six-ingredient cap keeps modified versions of complicated recipes within the realm of possibility, while the limit on house-made syrups promises less time spent at the stove top and more time kicking back, Mai Tai in hand.

## Building the *Easy Tiki* Bar

At its most basic, the *Easy Tiki* bar requires only those core elements that comprise nearly every balanced tropical cocktail: sour, sweet, strong, weak, and (sometimes) spice. But there are countless ways to achieve each of those characteristics. Outlined here are suggestions for what to keep on hand—the hardworking ingredients that will allow you to churn out the greatest range of tropical cocktails with the least amount of effort and fewest possible bottles.

### Sour

Fresh-squeezed juices are the key to ticking the "sour" box. Store-bought options simply don't offer the same brightness, not to mention that they're typically laden with added sugars and preservatives, which can make them tough to balance with your own cocktail sweeteners. In fact, part of what made Don the Beachcomber's drinks stand out was his insistence on fresh citrus. Likewise, beginning in the 1970s, it was, in part, the turn away from fresh-squeezed juices in favor of concentrates and prepackaged options that contributed to the demise of tiki.

**LIME** —— Don the Beachcomber's favored citrus, lime, is the most called-for sour element in the tiki canon, perhaps because it works so well with a variety of base spirits, from gin to rum—in both aged and unaged expressions—as well as other citrus flavors, though it can easily stand alone.

**LEMON** —— Lemon is one of the components that Trader Vic introduced to the tiki palette, and modern bartenders continue to use it to add a jolt of acidity, even in recipes that didn't initially call for it. Scotty Schuder's updated Missionary's Downfall (page 64), for example, swaps the original lime for lemon to give extra brightness. While both lemon juice and lime juice contain similar levels of acid, the latter contains a blend of citric and malic acids, while the former contains only citric acid, which gives it the characteristic citrus tang that works especially well with unaged spirits and in conjunction with other juices.

**GRAPEFRUIT** —— Another favorite of Don the Beachcomber, grapefruit is almost always a supporting actor, whether it's tag-teaming with lime and orange juice or buttressing cinnamon syrup in Donn's Mix (page 157)—a winning flavor pairing that appears time and again in tiki cocktails both classic and modern.

**ORANGE** —— Don the Beachcomber only used orange juice in combination with grapefruit juice, and it does tend to require backup when acting as the sour element, since it lands on the less mouth-puckering end of the sour spectrum.

**PASSION FRUIT** —— Passion fruit has been a key player in the tiki palette since the Don the Beachcomber days. Central to the "exotic" flavor of Don's drinks, passion fruit is typically deployed in the form of a syrup, which adds both tanginess and sweetness, but it's a flavor that pairs exceptionally well with the rest of the core tiki ingredients, including rum, orgeat, and spice.

**PINEAPPLE** —— The only fruit that Don the Beachcomber employed that was not grown locally in Southern California, pineapple is a shortcut to that quintessential tropical flavor and, more than citrus, provides a fluffy texture to drinks.

## Sweet

Another arena where Donn Beach separated himself from traditional cocktail constructions was in his use of unusual sweeteners. His syrup repertoire extended well beyond just simple syrup to include ingredients that did double duty as both sweetening agents and flavoring tools. It was not uncommon for him to use maple syrup, honey, brown sugar, or grenadine, many of which are standard pantry items.

SIMPLE SYRUP —— The most basic of cocktail sweeteners, simple syrup generally consists of a one-to-one ratio of sugar to water and adds body as well as sweetness to any mixed drink (see page 159).

HONEY SYRUP —— Following the same construction as simple syrup, honey syrup is another straightforward sweetener, just with the added flavor of, well, honey (see page 155).

GRENADINE —— Essentially just pomegranate syrup, grenadine gets a bad rap thanks to the surplus of artificial examples littering the market, usually devoid of real pomegranate flavor. When made well, however, grenadine brings a deep red-fruit flavor that nicely complements aged rums (see page 157).

*Store-bought recommendations: Small Hand Foods grenadine, Jack Rudy Small Batch grenadine*

ORGEAT —— Perhaps Trader Vic's most important contribution to the tiki palette, orgeat is an almond milk syrup, sometimes doctored with orange flower water, that is creamy, nutty, and velvety all at once and has become a quintessential tiki flavor (see page 158).

*Store-bought recommendation: Small Hand Foods orgeat, Orgeat Works Ltd T'Orgeat, Beachbum Berry's Latitude 29 Formula orgeat*

COCONUT CREAM —— A golden-age addition to the tiki palette, coconut cream is a valuable sweetener in the tiki arsenal, adding extra body and tropical flavor. While there are a number of store-bought examples of coconut cream, I recommend a simple house-made coconut cream instead (see page 156).

## Strong

As the native spirit of the tropics, rum is almost synonymous with tiki. But the category is one of the most diverse. It was precisely because of this variety, which differs depending on country of origin, distillation technique, and age statements, that Donn Beach experimented with mixing multiple rums within a single cocktail. Trader Vic, too, knew that different rums could significantly alter a drink, and he went so far as to suggest four different styles of the spirit (Cuban, Jamaican, Demerara, and Haitian) in his recipe books, while suggesting just one bottle or brand of every other spirit. To understand these stylistic differences in greater depth, turn to "Rum 101" on page 55. Here are four essential rums to keep handy.

AGED JAMAICAN RUM —— Aged Jamaican rums are responsible for bringing that recognizable "rum" quality as well as a characteristic overripe banana note to many cocktails, including the Zombie.

*Bottles to buy: Smith & Cross Jamaica rum, Appleton Estate Signature Blend Jamaican rum, Appleton Estate Reserve Blend Jamaican rum*

LIGHTLY AGED MARTINIQUE RUM —— Martinique rum is great at accentuating the nuttiness of orgeat, which can sometimes get lost in layered cocktails. Bottles with a little bit of age to them, often described as *élevé sous bois*, or simply gold or amber rum, provide a rounder mouthfeel and overall greater texture.

*Bottles to buy: Neisson Éleve Sous Bois, Rhum J.M Gold rum*

BLENDED UNAGED RUM —— One of the fastest-growing categories in rum today, blended unaged rums marry distillates from various countries of origin, creating layers of complexity in a single bottle and making them valuable workhorses in the tiki tool kit. Unaged expressions work great in Daiquiris and in conjunction with bolder aged rums.

*Bottles to buy: Plantation 3 Stars, Probitas White Blended rum*

OVERPROOF RUM —— Given its higher level of alcohol by volume, overproof rum, both aged and unaged, is key to cutting through the layers of citrus and syrups that make up so many tiki drinks.

*Bottles to buy: Plantation O.F.T.D., Wray & Nephew White Overproof rum*

# A WORD ON
## GARNISHES

Restraint has never been the name of the game in tiki; ostentation and excess have long been the calling card of the category, which introduced the idea of pineapples and coconuts as drinking vessels to a public accustomed to the surreptitious nature of Prohibition-era drinking.

Like an olive thrown into a Martini or a cherry into a Manhattan, garnish was never an afterthought for Don the Beachcomber, who used sculpted ice caves, geranium leaves, flowers, and lime hulls positioned to look like desert islands in a sea of pebbled ice to boost the theatricality of the entire tiki experience. His imitators only fanned the flames of the gonzo garnish trend, adding increasingly baroque elements to their signature drinks. The Mai-Kai, for example, was known for its Mystery Bowls—large-format cocktails that encircled a volcano made of ice, topped with a flaming lime shell. It was tiki, too, that gave rise to the nonutilitarian garnish—the paper umbrella and plastic swizzle stick—whose only purpose was to look cute and add to the impression of out-of-the-ordinariness.

Modern tiki bartenders have taken the garnish game to even greater heights. Dry ice is employed to mimic smoke, while bananas take on the likeness of dolphins or octopuses perched on the rims of elaborate tiki mugs. Actual figurines—pirates, zombies, mermaids—sometimes make an appearance.

*Easy Tiki* encourages this type of more-is-more approach when it comes to dressing your drink. Each recipe is accompanied by a suggested garnish, these should be read as exactly that: suggestions.

One of tiki's key dramatic flourishes comes by way of fire, that is, ignited lime hulls or cinnamon sticks placed atop the crushed ice of finished drinks. To achieve this effect, take a juiced lime hull, place it onto the drink, and pour overproof rum into the hollowed-out shell. Using a long match or lighter, ignite the liquid and then serve. Alternatively, place an overproof rum–soaked sugar cube in the hollowed-out lime shell and ignite the sugar cube, which will act as a wick and keep the flame alight.

When lighting a cinnamon stick, do so either before or after sticking it into the drink, but be sure to extinguish the flame prior to serving.

## Weak

The so-called weak component of tiki cocktails refers to dilution, primarily in the form of ice. But not all ice is created equal. Large, small, and cubed each offer their own advantages, which is why the recipes that follow call on a specific style for a particular result. These are suggestions for best results, but simply shaking or stirring with standard cubed ice, the sort you likely already have in your freezer, will still yield an imminently drinkable cocktail.

An easy rule of thumb to keep in mind is that the faster you want something to dilute, the smaller the ice you should use. This is why heady, concentrated mixtures such as the Zombie are typically served over crushed or pellet ice—they have the booze and body to withstand high amounts of dilution; in fact, they're designed to evolve and improve as the ice melts. For recipes that do not specify an amount of ice, cubed ice should be added to the cocktail shaker until it is three-quarters full.

CUBED ICE —— The standard cubed ice is a great go-to and is recommended for shaking and stirring cocktails when no particular effect (e.g., extra froth or less dilution) is sought.

LARGE ROCKS —— Large rocks, the type produced from oversize ice trays or bought premade in the store, offer the benefit of diluting more slowly than standard-size or cracked ice cubes, which means when used to shake a cocktail, they can agitate the mixture for a greater period of time, creating a frothier and colder drink without resulting in a watery cocktail.

CRUSHED ICE —— Also known as pellet or pebble ice, crushed ice will dilute when it's not packed together in an insulated ceramic tiki mug. Some bartenders will shake a drink with a few pellets to quickly chill and partially dilute it before it is served over more crushed ice. For at-home bartenders, you can crush ice with a Lewis bag and a mallet.

CRACKED ICE —— Created by breaking up large rocks or cubed ice with a muddler or other blunt instrument, cracked ice serves a similar purpose as crushed ice but is less uniform and typically larger than the latter, although considerably easier to produce.

## Spice

Spice was a secret weapon in Don the Beachcomber's arsenal. Whether in the form of liqueurs, syrups, bitters, or garnishes, spiced components gave his recipes great depth. In the syrups section starting on page 155, you'll find recipes for cinnamon syrup, Donn's Mix (a blend of cinnamon syrup and grapefruit juice), and ginger syrup, all of which bring the requisite spice to a given drink, but there are a number of other routes to incorporating spice into a cocktail.

**PIMENTO DRAM** —— Also known as allspice liqueur or allspice dram, this spiced liqueur has a pronounced baking spice profile, with cinnamon, clove, nutmeg, and, of course, allspice at the fore.

*Bottle to buy: St. Elizabeth allspice dram*

**FALERNUM** —— A rum-based liqueur that originated in Barbados, falernum, even in small amounts, adds depth and weight to cocktails with its vibrant blend of lime, spices, and almond flavor.

*Bottle to buy: John D. Taylor's velvet falernum*

**AROMATIC BITTERS** —— Aromatic bitters are only used in small doses but offer a concentrated form of conveying spice in tiki cocktails.

*Bottle to buy: Angostura bitters*

## Modifiers

It was, and remains, a common practice to build on the foundation ingredients with liqueurs and other spirits. Trader Vic in particular experimented with ingredients unheard of in the tropical realm, such as sweet and dry vermouths. Today, tiki recipes pull from an even greater array of modifiers, and it's not uncommon to see drinks featuring Italian amaro, sloe gin, cold-brew coffee, and more.

*Bottles to buy: Pierre Ferrand dry curaçao, Plantation Stiggins' Fancy pineapple rum, Giffard Banane du Brésil or Tempus Fugit crème de banane, absinthe*

## Tools

A standard bar kit—a cocktail shaker, jigger, mixing glass, spoon, and strainer—is all that's required to make the drinks in this book. There is one tool, however, that tiki bartenders both past and present swear by—though it's not required to make any of the drinks in these pages. A drink mixer, also known as a spindle blender, is the ultimate tiki secret weapon. Instructions for using a drink mixer, which is typically faster and more efficient than shaking, are supplied in all relevant recipes.

COCKTAIL SHAKER —— Cocktail shakers come in a variety of forms, but the most utilitarian example is the tin-on-tin type, which consists simply of two tins that fit together to form a vacuum seal, which allows for vigorous shaking without any leakage.

MIXING GLASS —— Spirit-forward formulas will likely get stirred in a mixing glass, a widemouthed tempered glass, or in a metallic vessel with ice, as they do not require air to be introduced into the mixture by shaking to achieve the proper texture.

HAWTHORNE STRAINER —— A Hawthorne strainer is identifiable by its circular springlike coil, which fits inside the mixing tin. When it comes time to strain the cocktail into a glass, a Hawthorne lets you control how much of the shaker contents are allowed into the glass.

FINE-MESH STRAINER —— Certain recipes call for "fine straining" or "double straining," which entails pouring the contents of a cocktail shaker first through a Hawthorne strainer and then through a fine-mesh strainer. Drinks that are shaken with fresh fruit or herbs typically require fine straining to catch any solid remnants.

JIGGER —— Precision is key for balances. It's best to have jiggers that can measure up to 2 ounces and in increments as small as ¼ ounce.

DRINK MIXER —— Faster and easier than using a cocktail shaker, the drink mixer precisely chills, dilutes, and aerates any cocktail that might otherwise be shaken. The Hamilton Beach DrinkMaster, an entry-level model, can be purchased for less than $40 and boasts a streamlined modern appearance that doubles as décor for any home tiki-bar setup.

# Batching for a Crowd

The consummate luau host never runs out of refreshments. To ensure that spirits remain high and glasses full, batch ahead when expecting a crowd. Though far from a perfect science, there are certain rules, like starting with the largest-volume ingredient and factoring in dilution, that will ensure any batched cocktail maintains the integrity of its single-serve counterpart. Here's a quick-and-dirty guide to group escapism.

## Start with the Largest-Volume Ingredient

To build your batch, I recommend beginning with the largest-volume ingredient, which is typically the base spirit. It's the smaller-volume ingredients, like citrus, sweetener, modifiers, and bitters, that have the highest margin for error. Even a drop too much of absinthe or other prominently flavored ingredient, for example, can easily throw a drink out of balance. So start big and then work down to small, adjusting for taste as you go.

## Avoid Scaling Up Aromatics or Bitters

Alcohol has a way of amplifying the potency of aromatics. As a rule of thumb, highly aromatic ingredients such as bitters, ginger juice, or ginger syrup should be introduced to the batch starting with half of what the recipe calls for and adjusted from there.

## Don't Forget About Dilution

Given the potency of tiki drinks, dilution is not to be overlooked. As with single-serve cocktails, about ½ ounce (1 tablespoon) water should be introduced to each serving by way of dilution. When making a single-serve recipe, this would come from either shaking the cocktail or stirring it with ice. For a large-format presentation, a shaken drink is best prediluted with water and then simply served over the rocks in individual glasses. For drinks designed to be served over crushed ice, less dilution is needed up front, as the melting ice provides dilution.

## Freeze-Ahead Stirred Drinks

To avoid standing behind the bar all night stirring cocktails to the proper dilution and temperature for guests, simply predilute a batch of your stirred cocktail and throw the whole thing in the freezer. When ready to drink, simply pour it into a coupe or cocktail glass. For spirituous recipes designed to be served up in a coupe, ¾ or 1 ounce (1½ or 2 tablespoons) water per serving can be added to the batch. If the drink is designed to be served on the rocks, you can add ¾ ounce water, or choose to forgo dilution altogether and simply pour the frozen batch into individual glasses over ice, which will dilute the drink for you.

In addition to meeting volume demands, freezing the cocktail ahead of time has the added benefit of providing a velvety mouthfeel while also reducing the "burn" that can sometimes accompany high-proof spirits, making the overall effect that of a more rounded cocktail.

### Be Careful with Sparkling Toppers, like Soda Water

When a recipe calls on a sparkling topper, like soda water, prosecco, or champagne, it's good practice to cut back on your initial dilution, as these components will bring their own water content to the mix. If you maintain the dilution of the base before adding these toppers, you risk their effervescence dissipating too quickly, resulting in a drink that is flat and too watery.

### Adjust to Taste

Taste your batch as you go along. Just like seasoning a dish, your batched cocktail should be adjusted to taste until the sour, sweet, strong, and weak elements are brought into balance.

## Rum 101

Rum is far and away the most diverse spirit category. Unlike whiskey, for example, which is likewise produced across the globe, rum lacks the sort of regulations that govern what can legally be deemed bourbon or rye. As such, rum varies drastically from country to country based on the raw materials used, which include molasses, sugarcane juice, and sugarcane syrup (or a combination); distillation type, either pot still or column still (or both); age, which ranges anywhere from unaged to aged more than twenty years; and type of finishing barrel, from sherry casks to zinfandel casks.

This diversity makes rum one of the most exciting spirits for mixing; it's what lends tiki its nuance and what inspires new tiki cocktails today. But it's also what makes the category one of the hardest to understand. It doesn't help that there has never been a consistent method for categorizing rum, adding another layer of opacity to this difficult-to-parse spirit.

Historically, rum has been broken out into categories based on the colonizing country of the rum-producing region: Spanish-style, English-style, French-style. Needless to say, this is an outdated method that does little to distinguish between the nuances of rum made in Jamaica and that made in Martinique, for example. More modern methods of categorization will sometimes divide rums by color (light, gold, dark, black), which only takes into account a rum's age or distillation method. Here I've opted to divide the spirit by country of origin, which I find to be one of the most important factors in determining flavor profile.

A note on proof: Several of the suggested bottles will be designated "overproof." This refers to their alcohol by volume (ABV), and certain tiki cocktails will recommend an overproof rum, whether aged or unaged, to bolster the backbone of a recipe.

## Jamaican

Aged Jamaican rum, those that have typically rested in a barrel between two and eight years, can run the gamut from more refined expressions based on a combination of column- and pot-distilled spirit, like Appleton Estate, to those characterized by their funky profile (the product of longer fermentation periods and pot-still production) often defined by an aroma of overripe banana (known as "funk" or "hogo"). Unaged Jamaican rum likewise possesses an overripe banana aroma, is typically bottled at a higher proof (126 proof), and is often used to lend backbone to a cocktail in combination with the bolder-flavored aged expressions.

UNAGED —— Wray & Nephew (overproof), Hampden Estate Rum Fire (overproof)

AGED —— Appleton Estate Signature Blend, Appleton Estate Reserve Blend, Doctor Bird, Smith & Cross, Hamilton Jamaican Pot-Still Gold, Hampden Estate Pure Single Jamaican

## Martinique

The majority of all rums on the market are molasses-based products. Martinique rums are the most notable outliers. Distilling these rums from sugarcane juice rather than sugarcane syrup or molasses gives them a distinctive grassy, dry profile. Martinique rums are also among the most restricted rums in the world, thanks to their AOC designation. Short for Appellation d'Origine Contrôlée, the AOC dictates irrigation periods, maximum harvest yields, distillation method, and more. Because Martinique is a French island, these rums are typically referred to as *rhum agricole*, which translates to "agricultural rum." However, the "rhum agricole" label does not necessarily indicate that a rum is from Martinique or the French Caribbean, as other rums distilled from sugarcane juice might bear the label but are not governed by the AOC. Unaged expressions tend to be dry and funky, perfect for a Daiquiri, while aged expressions offer a rounder mouthfeel that works well in a Mai Tai.

UNAGED —— Neisson Rhum Agricole Blanc, Rhum Clément Premiére Canne, Rhum Clément Canne Bleue, Rhum J.M Blanc

AGED —— Rhum J.M Gold, Neisson Élevé Sous Bois, Rhum Clément Select Barrel

## Haiti

Though Haiti does not produce very many rums, the few brands it does manufacture cover a wide range of flavor profiles: on one end of the spectrum are the more refined expressions, which are distilled from a mixture of sugarcane juice and sugarcane syrup, yielding a drier, less earthy profile compared to the 100 percent sugarcane-juice variety of Haitian rum, better known as clairin. The most notable and widely available example of the former is Barbancourt rum, a non-AOC rhum agricole finished in French oak barrels, which brings a tannic quality to cocktails. Clairin, on the other hand, distilled from indigenous varietals of sugarcane, is prized for its distinctive, bold body that differs even from rhum agricole produced on nearby Martinique.

UNAGED —— Rhum Barbancourt Blanc, Clairin Sajous

AGED —— Rhum Barbancourt 4 year, Rhum Barbancourt 8 year

## Barbados Rum

Barbados rum is typically characterized by a blend of pot- and column-distilled rums, resulting in full-bodied expressions that tend to be drier and less funky than certain other Caribbean rums.

UNAGED —— St. Nicholas Abbey White, Mount Gay Eclipse

AGED —— St. Nicholas Abbey 5 year, Mount Gay Black Barrel

## Guyana

Guyanese rum is more typically referred to as Demerara rum. These are richer, fuller-bodied rums defined by a distinctive smokiness on the palate. Unlike rums from other origins, Guyanese expressions are all aged a minimum of three years. In tiki cocktails, these rums can add richness in the texture, not unlike brown sugar, and baking spice notes to the palette.

AGED —— El Dorado 8, El Dorado 12, Hamilton 86, Hamilton 151 (overproof), Lemon Hart & Son 151 (overproof)

## Puerto Rico

These rums are the lightest and driest on the market. Produced on multicolumn stills, the resulting spirit is more neutral than many pot-stilled rums. In aged expressions, Puerto Rican rum displays a strong oakiness from the barrels in which it rests. These rums are typically used as a base spirit in conjunction with more complex ones to keep those flavors from overpowering the drink. In short, it offers dryness rather than perceived sweetness.

UNAGED —— Bacardí Carta Blanca, Don Q Cristal

AGED —— Bacardí Ocho, Don Q Añejo, Ron del Barrilito 3 Star

## Domestic Rum

Within the last decade, domestic rum has seen a significant uptick in production across the United States. Largely lead by craft distillers in Southern states and along the Eastern Seaboard, the only unifying characteristic is a tendency toward experimentation, in both the raw materials used in the distillation process and the barrels in which the spirits are aged.

**UNAGED** —— Privateer Silver Reserve, Kō Hana Hawaiian Agricole

**AGED** —— Privateer True American Amber, Thomas Tew Dark, High Wire Low Country Agricole

## Blends

It's common practice for bars to have their own house blends of rum, created by mixing expressions of their choice into a single bottle. It's a practice that has its roots with (yes, you guessed it) Don the Beachcomber. Today, the rum category has exploded to such a degree that a number of brands have started to bottle their own blends from various countries. These bottles are hardworking spirits that can achieve the effect of anywhere from three to five rums in a single bottle.

**UNAGED** —— Plantation 3 Stars, Probitas, Banks 5 Island Blend

**AGED** —— Denizen Merchant's Reserve, Plantation O.F.T.D. (overproof)

## Black Rum

Characterized by the addition of molasses or caramel (or both), black rum is the only rum it makes sense to describe by color, as its distillation method, country of origin, and age can vary. In other words, color is the *only* unifying trait of this rum. Rarely called on by itself, black rum is typically a tool for adding richer mouthfeel.

**EXAMPLE** —— Hamilton Jamaican Pot Still Black

## Spiced Rum

It should be noted that none of tiki's classic recipes employed spiced rum; but in the Caribbean, the practice of infusing rum with various spices to one's own specifications dates back as far as rum itself. Today, a number of craft distilleries have produced bottled versions that have inevitably found their way into the modern tiki repertoire, as they add a flavorful kick to any cocktail.

**EXAMPLES** —— Chairman's Reserve, Sailor Jerry, Don Q oak barrel spiced

# CLASSIC RECIPES

The twenty recipes that follow, drawn from the works of Don the Beachcomber and Trader Vic, aim to capture the simpler—but not simplistic—side of tiki. While what follows are not, in every instance, faithful interpretations of historic recipes, at their core, they capture the escapism and fantasy that only tiki can achieve.

# DONGA PUNCH

PAUL MCGEE, LOST LAKE, CHICAGO

Jeff "Beachbum" Berry first discovered this 1937 recipe in the handwritten notebook of Dick Santiago, an original Don the Beachcomber maître d', which was gifted to him by Santiago's daughter Jennifer. The book was written in code, and Berry spent several years deciphering precisely what Donn's Mix contained, before ultimately discovering it to be a mixture of grapefruit juice and cinnamon syrup, a flavor combination that remains popular in tiki recipes today. Here, Paul McGee makes only one minor tweak to the minimal recipe by bumping up the rum component by half an ounce for a more pronounced backbone.

---

2 ounces aged Martinique rum (preferably Neisson Élevé Sous Bois)

1½ ounces Donn's Mix (page 157)

¾ ounce lime juice

---

GARNISH   grapefruit peel, cinnamon stick, edible orchid, mint

Combine all the ingredients in a cocktail shaker and add ½ cup crushed ice. Shake for 5 seconds. Pour into a tall glass or tiki mug and top with more crushed ice. Garnish with a grapefruit peel, cinnamon stick, edible orchid, and mint.

VARIATION   Combine the liquid ingredients in a drink mixer tin with 1 cup crushed ice. Buzz for 3 seconds. Pour into a tall glass or tiki mug, top with crushed ice, and garnish as directed.

# ZOMBIE

JEFF "BEACHBUM" BERRY, LATITUDE 29, NEW ORLEANS

Don the Beachcomber's ten-ingredient Zombie is one of the most storied cocktails in the tiki canon. Like many of the Beachcomber's recipes, its contents were a mystery until Jeff "Beachbum" Berry decoded its cryptic ingredients, but its potency was legendary from the start. Customers who visited any Beachcomber outpost were limited to two per sitting, a mandate that helped shape the lore of this drink. In 2007, Berry created this simplified rendition, of which he says, "While nowhere near as layered and complex as Don the Beachcomber's ten-ingredient original, my bare-bones version does approximate its flavor profile, without sending you on a scavenger hunt for 151-proof Lemon Hart rum, falernum, a blender, or crushed ice."

1 ounce aged Jamaican rum

½ ounce overproof aged Puerto Rican rum (preferably Don Q)

½ ounce cinnamon syrup (page 156)

1 ounce white grapefruit juice

¾ ounce lime juice

GARNISH   mint sprig

Combine all the ingredients in a cocktail shaker. Add ice and shake until chilled, about 10 seconds. Pour into a tall glass, adding more ice to fill if necessary. Garnish with a mint sprig.

# MISSIONARY'S DOWNFALL

SCOTTY SCHUDER, DIRTY DICK, PARIS

Pineapple and mint are the stars of the show in this widely imitated Don the Beachcomber recipe from the 1940s. At the Paris tiki den Dirty Dick, owner Scotty Schuder—who sports a bicep-size tattoo of Donn's likeness—doesn't stray far from the original. Schuder simply swaps lime juice for the higher acidity of lemon and dials back the honey mix, making up the sweetness with the concentrated flavor of crème de pêche.

---

1¼ ounces unaged blended rum (preferably Plantation 3 Stars)

½ ounce honey syrup (page 155)

½ ounce crème de pêche (preferably Merlet crème de pêche de vigne)

¾ ounce lemon juice

5 (1-inch) pineapple cubes

6 mint leaves

---

GARNISH  pineapple wedge, mint bouquet, confectioners' sugar, edible orchid

Combine all the ingredients in a blender with ¾ cup ice and process until smooth. Pour into a snifter glass. Garnish with a pineapple wedge, a mint bouquet, a dusting of confectioners' sugar, and an edible orchid.

# SHAKEN MISSIONARY'S DOWNFALL

JELANI JOHNSON, CLOVER CLUB, BROOKLYN

In this shaken alternative to the blended Missionary's Downfall (facing page), Jelani Johnson ups the rum quotient by a full ounce from Don's original recipe, likewise upping the lime, but dialing back the sweeter components, like peach liqueur and honey syrup. Served over crushed ice, the amped-up drink evolves over the course of enjoying it.

10 mint leaves

2 ounces unaged blended rum

¾ ounce lime juice

¾ ounce pineapple juice

½ ounce peach liqueur (preferably G.E. Massenez crème de pêche)

½ ounce honey syrup (page 155)

GARNISH   mint sprigs

Combine all the ingredients in a cocktail shaker. Add ice and shake until chilled, about 10 seconds. Strain into a tiki mug and top with crushed ice. Garnish with mint sprigs.

# DEMERARA DRY FLOAT

JANE DANGER, NEW YORK

The Demerara Dry Float is a classic Don the Beachcomber recipe that pairs rich-bodied rum with the flavors that show it off best—passion fruit and citrus. In Jane Danger's version, a half ounce of unaged blended rum bolsters the heady base, while overproof Demerara rum provides the signature finish.

¾ ounce Demerara rum (preferably El Dorado 3 year)

½ ounce unaged blended rum (preferably Banks 5 Island Blend)

¾ ounce lime juice

½ ounce passion fruit syrup (page 159)

⅜ ounce maraschino liqueur (preferably Luxardo)

½ ounce overproof Demerara rum (preferably Lemon Hart & Son 151)

GARNISH  lime shell soaked in overproof Demerara rum

Combine all the ingredients except the overproof rum in a cocktail shaker. Add 1 large cracked ice cube and shake until it melts. Pour into a tumbler and top with more cracked ice and the overproof rum. Garnish with a rum-soaked lime shell and light it with a long match or kitchen lighter just before serving.

# COBRA'S FANG

PATRICK GARTNER, DONNA, BROOKLYN

The original Don the Beachcomber Cobra's Fang from the 1930s called on a high-proof Demerara rum in addition to a pot-stilled Jamaican rum. In this streamlined take, Patrick Gartner notes that you can get a similar ABV, "funk," and barrel flavor just by using Smith & Cross Jamaican rum. Likewise, instead of using both falernum and Angostura bitters, Gartner achieves a baking spice note and a rich nuttiness with the addition of Swedish punsch, a versatile Nordic liqueur. The combination of passion fruit and grenadine, meanwhile, provides a fruity, zesty through line.

---

2 ounces aged Jamaican rum (preferably Smith & Cross)

1½ ounces orange juice

½ ounce passion fruit syrup (page 159)

¼ ounce grenadine (page 157)

¼ ounces Swedish punsch (preferably Kronan)

2 dashes absinthe (preferably Pernod)

---

GARNISH   mint sprig, orange twist

Combine all the ingredients in a cocktail shaker. Add ice and shake until chilled, about 10 seconds. Strain into a snifter glass and top with crushed ice. Garnish with a mint sprig and an orange twist.

# DON'S SPECIAL DAIQUIRI

DANIELE DALLA POLA, ESOTICO, MIAMI

The original Don's Special Daiquiri is a 1970s update to a 1930s variant known as the Mona Daiquiri. When Don the Beachcomber first created the Mona in 1934, he called on a base of thirty-year-old Myers's Mona Rum—for which the drink is named—and further amended the formula with the addition of both passion fruit and honey syrups. Following the discontinuation of Mona rum in 1946, the Beachcomber, true to his personal mantra that what one rum can't do, several can, altered the recipe by using a blend of Jamaican gold and Puerto Rican light rums for what came to be known as Don's Special Daiquiri. In this version, Daniele Dalla Pola swaps in agave nectar for honey syrup and makes the unorthodox addition of spiced rum for an extra kick.

---

1 ounce aged Puerto Rican rum (preferably Bacardí Ocho)

½ ounce aged Jamaican rum (preferably Plantation)

½ ounce spiced rum

¾ ounce agave nectar

½ ounce frozen passion fruit purée (preferably The Perfect Purée of Napa Valley)

½ ounce lime juice

---

Combine all the ingredients in a cocktail shaker. Add ice and shake until chilled, about 10 seconds. Strain into a coupe.

# PEARL DIVER

GABY MLYNARCZYK, ACCOMPLICE BAR, LOS ANGELES

The Pearl Diver is Don the Beachcomber's iced take on hot buttered rum. Key to its construction is a proprietary mixture known as Gardenia Mix—an amalgam of honey, butter, and spiced syrups. In Gaby Mlynarczyk's version of the mix, far fewer ingredients are required, and browned butter, rather than simply softened butter, lends a slightly savory note.

---

1½ ounces unaged blended rum (preferably Denizen)

1 ounce mango brandy (preferably Rhine Hall)

1 ounce Gardenia Mix (page 155)

1 barspoon Jamaican rum (preferably Smith & Cross)

½ ounce simple syrup (page 159)

½ ounce lime juice

---

GARNISH   mango leaf, edible orchid, freshly grated nutmeg

Combine all the ingredients in a cocktail shaker. Add a few small pieces of ice and shake until they melt. Pour into a Pearl Diver glass or a glass of your choice. Top with crushed ice. Garnish with a mango leaf, an edible orchid, and some freshly grated nutmeg.

# NUI NUI

BRIAN MILLER, NEW YORK

Like so many of Don the Beachcomber's recipes, the Nui Nui evaded discovery by modern bartenders until Jeff "Beachbum" Berry unearthed the contents of Donn's Spices #2, a vanilla-allspice mixture commonly called for across the Beachcomber's drink output. Here Brian Miller, a self-proclaimed "tiki pirate," hews closely to the original, simply calling on a touch more syrup and a dash of absinthe rather than Angostura bitters.

---

2 ounces Demerara rum (preferably El Dorado 5 year)

½ ounce orange juice

½ ounce lime juice

¼ ounce Donn's Spices #2 (page 157)

¼ ounce cinnamon syrup (page 156)

¼ ounce cane syrup (see simple syrup variation, page 159)

---

GARNISH  1 continuous orange peel from an entire orange, absinthe

Combine all the ingredients in a cocktail shaker. Add 4 ice cubes and shake until chilled, about 10 seconds. Strain into a footed Pilsner glass filled with crushed ice. Garnish with a continuous orange peel from an entire orange and a dash of absinthe.

# PUKA-PUKA PUNCH

JANE DANGER, NEW YORK

Likely named after *The Book of Puka-Puka: A Lone Trader on a South Seas Atoll* by Robert Dean Frisbie, Puka-Puka Punch is a baroque concoction consisting of multiple rums, myriad tropical juices, and syrups. To keep the ingredient list down, Jane Danger omits falernum and calls on two bottles of blended rum to do the work of several.

1 ounce blended aged rum (preferably Plantation O.F.T.D.)

1 ounce blended unaged rum (preferably Banks 5 Island Blend)

¾ ounce orange juice

¾ ounce lime juice

¾ ounce passion fruit syrup (page 159)

½ ounce honey syrup (page 155)

GARNISH  **mint sprigs, Angostura bitters**

Combine all the ingredients in a blender with 1 cup cracked ice and blend for 5 seconds. Pour into a snifter and garnish with mint sprigs and 2 dashes of Angostura bitters. Serve with a straw.

# TRADER VIC'S GROG

MARTIN CATE, SMUGGLER'S COVE, SAN FRANCISCO

In Martin Cate's reinterpreted Trader Vic's Grog, he ups the bitter quotient with additional dashes of Angostura bitters. "This was a popular drink with staff and industry when I bartended at Trader Vic's," says Cate. "It achieves a satisfying depth and richness with a short ingredient list." Cate's recipe relies on a full ounce of lemon juice, but he notes that if a less tart drink is preferred, this quantity can easily be dialed back to taste.

---

2 ounces aged Jamaican or Demerara rum, or aged overproof rum (see Note)

1 ounce lemon juice (less if a sweeter taste is preferred)

1 ounce pineapple juice

1 ounce passion fruit syrup (see page 159)

2 or 3 dashes Angostura bitters

---

GARNISH   maraschino cherries on a cocktail spear, mint sprig

Combine all the ingredients in a cocktail shaker with ice. Shake for about 5 seconds. Strain into a footed Pilsner glass. Fill with crushed ice and garnish with maraschino cherries on a cocktail spear and a mint sprig.

VARIATION   Combine all the ingredients in a drink mixer with 1 cup crushed ice and buzz for 3 seconds. Pour the contents into a footed Pilsner glass and garnish with maraschino cherries on a cocktail spear and a mint sprig.

NOTE   Recommended rums include Coruba, Smith & Cross, Plantation O.F.T.D., Hamilton 151, Hamilton 86, and Lemon Hart & Son 151.

# SCORPION

JANE DANGER, NEW YORK

The Scorpion dates back to the 1950s and was traditionally a drink to be shared, hence the well-known vessel, the Scorpion Bowl. With its large-format presentation, Jane Danger's version stays true to the sharable nature of the original, though it can be scaled down to a single serving as well. If cognac is unavailable, apple brandy works well, too.

2¼ ounces lime juice

3 ounces orange juice

2¼ ounces orgeat (page 158)

2 ounces cognac

2 ounces unaged blended rum (preferably Plantation 3 Stars)

2 ounces aged Puerto Rican rum (preferably Ron Del Barrilito Especial 3 Star)

GARNISH  lime shell soaked in overproof rum, lime and orange half-wheels

Combine all the ingredients in a blender with 1 cup cubed ice. Blend for 10 seconds and then pour into a Scorpion Bowl or other large vessel. Garnish with a rum-soaked lime shell and lime and orange half-wheels, then set the lime shell aflame with a long match or kitchen lighter just before serving.

# MAI TAI

MARTIN CATE, SMUGGLER'S COVE, SAN FRANCISCO

Perhaps the most iconic cocktail that Trader Vic ever created, the Mai Tai has gone through several iterations according to shifting availabilities of various rums since its genesis in 1944. Vic originally called for a seventeen-year-old Jamaican rum, but the sheer popularity of the drink at his rapidly expanding empire resulted in a dwindling supply of that particular bottling. The years that followed witnessed several reformulations based on available rums, but Martin Cate notes that this hardly impacted the end result. "The fundamental nature of the Mai Tai is that it's a showcase for great rum to shine. All the other ingredients are in small, supporting roles," he says, adding, "the perfect rum or rum combination for the Mai Tai is the one that makes you happiest when you drink it."

---

2 ounces aged Jamaican rum or other full-bodied, "unapologetic" rum (see Note)

½ ounce orange curaçao

¾ ounce lime juice

¼ ounce rich Demerara syrup (page 158)

¼ ounce orgeat (page 158)

---

GARNISH  lime shell, mint sprig

Combine all the ingredients in a cocktail shaker. Add 1½ cups crushed ice and a few standard ice cubes. Shake until frost appears on the shaker and then pour into a double Old-Fashioned glass. Garnish with an upside-down lime shell and a mint sprig.

NOTE  Recommended rums include Appleton Estate Rare Blend, Coruba, and Denizen Merchant's Reserve.

# FOG CUTTER

PAUL MCGEE, LOST LAKE, CHICAGO

In signature Trader Vic fashion, the Fog Cutter calls on a blend of three different base spirits (gin, cognac, rum) and a float of sherry. With so many different profiles competing, it's a drink that can be difficult to balance. In the version Paul McGee serves at Lost Lake in Chicago, he tilts the axis of the drink more toward rum, in this case a lightly aged rhum agricole from Martinique rather than the "light rum" originally called for. A slightly amended version appears below, which simply loses the orange curaçao in favor of a hefty spritz of orange oil over the surface of the drink.

---

1 ounce aged Martinique rum (preferably Neisson Élevé Sous Bois)

½ ounce cognac

½ ounce London dry gin

¾ ounce orgeat (page 158)

½ ounce amontillado sherry

1 ounce lemon juice

---

GARNISH   orange peel, mint bouquet, edible orchid, swizzle stick

Combine all ingredients in a cocktail shaker and add 1 cup crushed ice. Shake for 5 seconds. Pour into a tiki mug and top with another cup of crushed ice. Express an orange peel's oils over the cocktail, then twirl the peel into a floret. Garnish with the floret, a mint bouquet, edible orchid, and swizzle stick.

VARIATION   Combine the liquid ingredients in a drink mixer tin with 1 cup crushed ice. Buzz for 3 seconds. Pour into a tiki mug, top with another cup of crushed ice, and garnish as directed.

# MARTINIQUE SWIZZLE

GARRET RICHARD, EXISTING CONDITIONS, NEW YORK

In Garret Richard's adaptation of Trader Vic's swizzle, the New York–based bartender splits the rum component between the expected Martinique rum and a fuller-bodied blended expression that combines distillates from both Barbados and Guyana. He notes that an aged Martinique rum could be substituted for an even richer variation. Though it's not mandatory, he suggests adding a pinch of salt to make each flavor pop.

---

1 ounce unaged Martinique rum (preferably Trois Rivières Cuvée de l'Océan)

1 ounce aged blended rum (preferably Dos Maderas 5+5)

¾ ounce lime juice

¾ ounce cane syrup (see simple syrup variation, page 155) or Rhum J.M Sirop de Sucre de Canne

½ teaspoon absinthe (preferably Pernod)

2 dashes Angostura bitters

---

GARNISH   freshly grated nutmeg, freshly grated cinnamon, mint sprig, lime twist

Combine all the ingredients in a small Collins or Pilsner glass. Fill the glass with crushed ice and swizzle using a swizzle stick or barspoon. Garnish with freshly grated nutmeg, freshly grated cinnamon, mint, and a lime twist.

# SHINGLE STAIN

DAVID KINSEY, KINDRED, SAN DIEGO

While later versions of Trader Vic's Shingle Stain dropped the pimento dram and added both cranberry and pine-apple juices, David Kinsey's interpretation harkens back to the original. The deep red-fruit flavors of the grenadine harmonize with the richness of aged Jamaican rum, while pimento dram and Angostura bitters bring a pronounced baking spice note, for endless layers of complexity.

---

| | |
|---|---|
| 1 ounce aged Jamaican rum | ½ ounce grenadine (page 157) |
| ¾ ounce unaged or lightly aged Martinique rum | ¼ ounce pimento dram (preferably St. Elizabeth) |
| ½ ounce lime juice | 2 dashes Angostura bitters |

---

GARNISH   mint sprig

Combine all the ingredients in a cocktail shaker. Add ice and shake until chilled, about 10 seconds. Strain into a Zombie glass and top with cracked or crushed ice until full. Garnish with a mint sprig.

# SIBONEY

ANTONIO MARTINEZ, BOOTLEGGER TIKI, PALM SPRINGS

First appearing in Trader Vic's 1974 book *Rum Cookery & Drinkery*, here the Siboney is updated by Antonio Martinez to be more rum-forward with an additional half ounce of Jamaican rum as the base. Martinez also doubles down on pineapple, which appears in fresh juice form and in the form of pineapple rum. The result is a modernized take that's bursting with tropical fruit flavor.

---

1½ ounces aged Jamaican rum (preferably Doctor Bird)

½ ounce Plantation Stiggins' Fancy pineapple rum

1 ounce pineapple juice

¾ ounce lime juice

½ ounce passion fruit syrup (page 159)

½ ounce rich Demerara syrup (page 158)

---

Combine all the ingredients in a cocktail shaker. Add ice and shake until chilled, about 10 seconds. Strain into a coupe or cocktail glass.

# TRADER VIC'S SOUR

JELANI JOHNSON, CLOVER CLUB, BROOKLYN

Trader Vic created a number of variations on the sour, which call on various base spirits and a variety of different types of citrus. Here, Jelani Johnson offers a template that works equally well with bourbon, Scotch, or brandy as the base.

---

**2 ounces bourbon, Scotch, or brandy**

**¾ ounce lemon juice**

**½ ounce orgeat (page 158)**

**¼ ounce simple syrup (page 159)**

---

GARNISH   **edible orchid, flag**

Combine all the ingredients in a cocktail shaker. Add ice and shake until chilled, about 10 seconds. Strain into a double rocks glass filled with ice. Garnish with an orchid and a flag.

# LONDON SOUR

JANE DANGER AND AUSTIN HARTMAN, PARADISE LOUNGE, NEW YORK

Trader Vic's London Sour was originally built on a Scotch base. Here, Jane Danger and Austin Hartman expand the template to accommodate a spirit rarely seen in the early days of tiki: mezcal. Modified with small measure of manzanilla sherry in addition to the expected citrus and orgeat, the recipe serves as a reminder of the timelessness of the tiki canon.

1 orange wedge
(about ¼ orange)

1½ ounces mezcal
(preferably Del Maguey Vida)

¾ ounce lemon juice

½ ounce manzanilla sherry
(preferably Barbadillo)

½ ounce orgeat (page 158)

½ ounce passion fruit syrup
(page 159)

GARNISH    thin spiral of lemon peel

Put the orange wedge in a cocktail shaker and muddle to release its oils and juice. Add all the remaining ingredients and ice and shake until chilled, about 10 seconds. Fine strain (see "fine-mesh strainer," page 51) into a rocks glass filled with ice. Garnish with a thin spiral of lemon peel.

# EASTERN SOUR

JEFF "BEACHBUM" BERRY, LATITUDE 29, NEW ORLEANS

"Trader Vic's original circa-1960s Eastern Sour is not a complicated drink," says Jeff "Beachbum" Berry, "but this quicker and easier version eliminates one ingredient and takes the vagueness out of the original spec, which somewhat imprecisely called for the juice of half an orange and half a lemon, ignoring the fact that oranges and lemons come in all different sizes." In other words, it's the quintessential *Easy Tiki* cocktail.

---

| | |
|---|---|
| 1½ ounces bourbon | ½ ounce lemon juice |
| 1 ounce orange juice | ¼ ounce orgeat (page 158) |

---

GARNISH    spiral-cut orange and lemon twists, tied into knots

Combine all the ingredients in a cocktail shaker. Add ice and shake until chilled, about 10 seconds. Strain into a rocks glass over 1 large ice cube. Garnish with tied spiral-cut orange and lemon twists.

# MODERN RECIPES

The ingredients available to the bartender today have allowed modern tiki recipes to expand the boundaries of the genre well beyond those established during tiki's golden age. In the pages that follow, you'll find recipes that call on everything from sloe gin to Italian amaro, but the common thread linking them all together is a transportive quality that ties them to Don the Beachcomber's and Trader Vic's original concoctions. Tropical, refreshing, and made with six ingredients or fewer, this is what Easy Tiki looks like.

# LOST VOYAGE

MICHAEL KOTKE, FOUNDATION TIKI BAR, MILWAUKEE

At Foundation Tiki Bar in Milwaukee, bartender Michael Kotke has been serving tiki classics alongside a menu of original South Seas–inspired cocktails for years. His Lost Voyage comes from their latest menu and builds on a split base of aged Martinique rum and amontillado sherry, a pairing that lends a dryness to the drink, while cinnamon syrup adds depth, and both lemon and orange juices contribute their signature citrus kick.

1½ ounces aged Martinique rum (preferably Rhum Clément Select Barrel)

1½ ounces amontillado sherry (preferably Lustau)

1 ounce cinnamon syrup (page 156)

1 ounce lemon juice

1 ounce orange juice

1 teaspoon Angostura bitters

GARNISH   orange slice, mint sprig

Combine the Martinique rum, sherry, cinnamon syrup, lemon juice, and orange juice in a cocktail shaker and shake briefly without ice. Fill a 16-ounce Collins glass with crushed ice. Pour the cocktail into the glass and top with more crushed ice until the glass is full. Pour the bitters over the top of the cocktail and garnish with an orange slice and a mint sprig.

# IMPROVED BAJAN RUM PUNCH

AUSTIN HARTMAN, PARADISE LOUNGE, NEW YORK

"The Bajan Rum Punch is an island staple," says Austin Hartman, owner of New York's Paradise Lounge, "but everyone has their own twist or pop to it." Here Hartman builds depth and complexity with the additions of spicy ginger syrup and aromatic nutmeg to the classic formula that dictates all the punches: one of sour, two of sweet, three of strong, four of weak. "Through my various travels [to Barbados], and many rum punches later, this is my favorite spec," he says. "Aside from the one at the Beach Shack in Speightstown, Barbados."

2 ounces Barbados rum (preferably Mount Gay Black Barrel)

1 ounce ginger syrup (page 156)

¾ ounce lime juice

2 dashes Angostura bitters

1 ounce soda water

GARNISH    freshly grated nutmeg

Combine the rum, ginger syrup, lime juice, and bitters in a cocktail shaker. Add ice and shake until chilled, about 10 seconds. Strain into a Collins or hurricane glass filled with ice and top with the soda water. Garnish with freshly grated nutmeg.

# QUARANTINE ORDER

WILLIAM PRESTWOOD, PAGAN IDOL, SAN FRANCISCO

Building off the quintessential flavor combination created by Don the Beachcomber, William Prestwood marries cinnamon and grapefruit with passion fruit, lime, Angostura bitters, and heady Jamaican rum in his Quarantine Order. "I wanted to create a drink that could highlight the cinnamon notes in Angostura bitters," says Prestwood. "I added some lime, passion fruit, and my favorite rums for mixing," he says, citing the blend of Appleton Estate Signature and Rum-Bar Gold, a go-to mixture his team has since dubbed "Jam Tropics."

3 ounces aged Jamaican rum (preferably equal parts Appleton Estate Signature and Rum-Bar Gold)

1 ounce lime juice

1 ounce grapefruit juice

½ ounce cinnamon syrup (page 156)

½ ounce passion fruit syrup (page 159)

5 dashes Angostura bitters

GARNISH   mint sprig, cherry, lime wheel

Combine all the ingredients in a cocktail shaker. Add ice and shake vigorously until the ice breaks up into smaller pieces, about 30 seconds. Pour into a snifter and garnish with a mint sprig and a cherry speared through a lime wheel.

# PARADISE LOST

KIRK ESTOPINAL, CANE & TABLE, NEW ORLEANS

"I wanted something tiki, but of the moment," says Kirk Estopinal of his Paradise Lost recipe. Inspired by the Green Isaac Special created by cocktail historian Philip Greene, Estopinal's twist swaps in vodka for gin and adds the decidedly tropical combination of lime, coconut water, and orgeat, complemented by an ounce of dry fino sherry. "Refreshing, healing, and light—this drink is all those things," says Estopinal.

---

1 ounce vodka

1 ounce coconut water

1 ounce fino sherry

¾ ounce lime juice

½ ounce orgeat (page 158)

---

GARNISH  2 dashes aromatic bitters, mint bouquet

Combine all the ingredients in a cocktail shaker. Add ice and shake until chilled, about 10 seconds. Strain into a Pilsner glass filled with crushed ice. Garnish with aromatic bitters and a mint bouquet.

# JUNIOR COLADA

DAVID PEREZ, LEI LOW, HOUSTON

"We were looking to create something that had a refreshing pop but still had the essence of a Piña Colada," says Russell Thoede, owner of Houston's Lei Low. "This drink is super easy to make, doesn't require any special ingredients, and doubles as a low-ABV drink as well," he notes. The sweetness of the formula can be adjusted depending on the type of coconut soda deployed—Coco Rico yields a sweetened version, while LaCroix's coconut-flavored sparkling water results in a drier take. At Lei Low, they often opt for carbonating coconut water in a soda siphon for optimum flavor.

---

1 ounce Plantation Stiggins' Fancy pineapple rum

½ ounce coconut liqueur (preferably Rhum Clément Mahina Coco)

1 ounce pineapple juice

¾ ounce lime juice

Coconut soda, to top

---

GARNISH   pineapple wedge, cocktail umbrella

Combine the rum, coconut liqueur, pineapple juice, and lime juice in a highball glass. Stir, using a swizzle stick or barspoon to combine. Add crushed ice and then top with coconut soda. Stir until well combined. Garnish with a pineapple wedge and a cocktail umbrella.

# ELUSIVE DREAMS

DEMI NATOLI, PATTERSON HOUSE, NASHVILLE

The Elusive Dreams, Demi Natoli's spin on Cuba's Hotel Nacional cocktail—rum, pineapple, lime, apricot—takes a decidedly tropical turn as she swaps out the apricot in favor of banana liqueur. Natoli then doubles down on the pineapple, using fresh pineapple juice and splitting the rum component between the traditional white rum and Plantation pineapple rum, which is infused with both the rind and fruit of Victoria pineapples. Cinnamon syrup provides a baking spice note for added depth and a nod to Don the Beachcomber's secret weapon.

---

1 ounce Plantation Stiggins' Fancy pineapple rum

1 ounce blended unaged rum (preferably Plantation 3 Stars)

1 ounce pineapple juice

¾ ounce lime juice

¾ ounce cinnamon syrup (page 156)

½ ounce banana liqueur (preferably Giffard Banane du Brésil)

---

GARNISH   pineapple wedge, edible orchid

Combine all the ingredients in a cocktail shaker. Add 1 large ice cube and shake until chilled, about 30 seconds. Strain through a fine-mesh strainer into a coupe and garnish with a pineapple crescent and an edible orchid.

# WISHFUL THINKING

JULIA MCKINLEY, CHICAGO

"This cocktail is concise and low-ABV but has all of the flavor of a classic tiki cocktail," says Julia McKinley, who cut her teeth at two of Chicago's most notable tiki bars, Three Dots and a Dash and Lost Lake. Here she deploys the classic tiki sensibility of combining disparate flavors to create a complex whole, but builds on a lower-proof sloe gin base. To this fruit-forward backbone, she adds the more traditional tiki flavors of ginger and Martinique rum to round out the cocktail.

---

2 ounces sloe gin
(preferably Hayman's)

1 ounce unaged Martinique rum
(preferably Rhum J.M Blanc)

1 ounce lime juice

1 ounce ginger syrup
(page 156)

3 dashes Angostura bitters

3 dashes absinthe

---

GARNISH   mint sprig

Combine all the ingredients in a cocktail shaker. Add cracked ice and shake until chilled, about 10 seconds. Pour into a decorative mug and add more cracked ice to fill, if necessary. Garnish with a mint sprig.

# IRON RANGER

ERICK CASTRO, POLITE PROVISIONS, SAN DIEGO

Erick Castro's Iron Ranger reads like a hybrid Don the Beachcomber and Trader Vic concoction. To a traditional 1930s Beachcomber build, Castro subs in a whiskey base, something favored by Trader Vic. The result is an imminently crushable tiki cooler, topped with an aromatic flourish of mint, a cinnamon stick, and freshly grated cinnamon.

2 ounces bourbon

1 ounce pineapple juice

¾ ounce lemon juice

½ ounce John D. Taylor's velvet falernum

½ ounce simple syrup (page 159)

2 dashes Angostura bitters

GARNISH   freshly grated cinnamon, cinnamon stick, mint sprig

Combine all the ingredients in a cocktail shaker. Add 1 large ice cube and shake until it melts. Pour into a hurricane glass and top with crushed ice. Garnish with freshly grated cinnamon, a cinnamon stick, and a mint sprig.

# MOJITO CRIOLLO NO. 1

PABLO MOIX, DAMA, LOS ANGELES

At Dama in Los Angeles, owner Pablo Moix demonstrates his penchant for Caribbean cocktails, the backbone of every tiki cocktail out there. His pared-down take on the Mojito expertly balances the sour (lime), sweet (sugar), strong (rum), and weak (sparkling water) of the classic tiki formula, while the fragrant addition of mint calls back to the Caribbean staple.

---

10 mint leaves

2 ounces unaged
Puerto Rican rum

1 ounce lime juice

2 barspoons sugar

3 ounces sparkling water

---

GARNISH   **mint sprig**

Put the mint leaves in a highball glass and muddle slightly. Add the rum, lime juice, sugar, and sparkling water and fill the glass with crushed ice. Stir with a barspoon to combine. Garnish with a mint sprig.

# OUR MAN IN HAVANA

GARRET RICHARD, EXISTING CONDITIONS, NEW YORK

Garret Richard's tikified take on the Cuban cocktail known as the El Presidente calls on nutty orgeat in place of grenadine and has a bittersweet aromatized wine stand in for the traditional white vermouth. By inverting the ratio of rum to aromatized wine, Richard's Our Man in Havana becomes a sessionable spin that can be enjoyed over the course of multiple rounds, without sacrificing complexity or body.

2 ounces Byrrh aromatized wine

1 ounce unaged Haitian rum (preferably Rhum Barbancourt 5 Star)

1 teaspoon dry orange curaçao

½ teaspoon orgeat (page 158)

1 dash Angostura bitters

1 dash orange bitters

GARNISH  spiraled thin lime twist

Combine all the ingredients in a mixing glass, fill with ice to within an inch of the rim, and stir to combine. Strain into a Nick & Nora glass and garnish with a spiraled lime twist.

# BALDWIN'S (EASY) SHERRY COLADA

RAN DUAN, BALDWIN BAR, BOSTON

At Baldwin Bar, located above Boston's Sichuan Garden restaurant, bartender Ran Duan serves his Sherry Colada, a mixture of palo cortado, manzanilla, and amontillado sherries, plus pineapple juice, house-made coconut cream, and lemon juice. Here he offers this "easy" version, which requires only one sherry—amontillado—cutting the ingredient list down to four without sacrificing craveability.

---

2 ounces amontillado sherry

1 ounce pineapple juice

1 ounce coconut cream (page 156)

¾ ounce lemon juice

---

GARNISH   pineapple wedge, pineapple fronds, Angostura bitters (optional)

Combine all the ingredients in a cocktail shaker. Add ice and shake until chilled, about 10 seconds. Pour into a Zombie or highball glass. Add crushed ice to fill the glass. Garnish with a pineapple wedge, pineapple fronds, and Angostura bitters, if desired.

# PRIVATEER

CHRIS VANDERGINST, MUTINY BAR, DETROIT

"I think this drink is a great example of where tiki is and where it's headed," says Chris Vanderginst. "I personally do not believe tiki should be this stagnant concept that is only one thing. It should evolve with the people and the community," he says of the ongoing evolution of the genre, which continues to embrace a variety of spirits outside the rum world. Here, tequila serves as the base spirit, complemented by passion fruit syrup, pineapple and lime juices, and a pinch of salt.

---

1½ ounces tequila

¾ ounce passion fruit syrup (page 159)

¾ ounce pineapple juice

½ ounce lime juice

Pinch of salt

---

GARNISH   torched rosemary sprig (See Note. For more tips on lighting garnishes on fire, see page 46.)

Combine all the ingredients in a cocktail shaker. Add ice and shake until chilled, about 10 seconds. Pour into a tiki mug, or double strain through a mesh strainer into a coupe. Garnish with a torched rosemary sprig.

NOTE   If serving in a tiki mug, singe the rosemary once it's been placed vertically in the glass; if serving in a coupe, singe the rosemary before placing it on the surface of the cocktail.

# THIRD WAVE SWIZZLE

RYAN LOTZ, SHORE LEAVE, BOSTON

Ryan Lotz describes his Third Wave Swizzle as "a tropical swizzle riff on the ubiquitous Espresso Martini." Cold-brew coffee concentrate supplies the requisite coffee kick, while gin is Lotz's base spirit of choice. In a nod to Don the Beachcomber, the recipe calls for a blend of two sweeteners, honey syrup and ginger syrup, which lends body to the thoroughly modern swizzle.

2 ounces gin

¾ ounce honey syrup
(page 155)

¾ ounce lemon juice

½ ounce cold-brew coffee concentrate

¼ ounce ginger syrup
(page 156)

GARNISH   lemon twist, grated coffee bean

Combine all the ingredients in a tall swizzle glass. Add crushed ice until the glass is full. Swizzle the drink with a swizzle stick or barspoon until the glass frosts. Garnish with a lemon twist and a grated coffee bean.

# SOMETHING TEQUILA

JOHN BERNARD, PORCO LOUNGE & TIKI ROOM, CLEVELAND

"All good tiki drinks have a great story behind them," says John Bernard, proprietor of Cleveland's Porco Lounge & Tiki Room. "Something Tequila was created in response to customers asking, 'Do you make Margaritas? Could you make me something tequila?'" In the Something Tequila, Bernard creates a hybrid of a Margarita and a Rum Barrel (a tiki classic) with a combination of three types of citrus, passion fruit, and tequila. While the agave-based spirit was not a typical twentieth-century tiki ingredient, Bernard impresses upon his guests that "tiki is all about the adventure and exploring what you like."

---

3 ounces tequila (preferably añejo)

1 ounce lime juice

1 ounce orange juice

1 ounce pineapple juice

1 ounce simple syrup (page 159)

½ ounce passion fruit syrup (page 159)

---

GARNISH   mint sprig, citrus wedges or wheels, edible flowers, swizzle sticks—whatever you have on hand

Combine all the ingredients in a cocktail shaker. Add ice and shake until chilled, about 10 seconds. Pour into a barrel-shaped tiki mug and garnish with mint, citrus wedges or wheels, flowers, and swizzle sticks.

# STAYCATION

DEVIN KENNEDY, POURING RIBBONS, NEW YORK

Devin Kennedy's Staycation offers a modernized, balanced interpretation of the 1970s-era Trade Winds cocktail, originally offered with a base of either rum or gin. Kennedy opts for rum, but splits it with a high-proof, spice-forward rye that's capable of standing up to the tropical and fruit-forward components. In addition to coconut and apricot, a splash of passion fruit amplifies the stone fruit notes. "This is a drink you have when you play ocean sounds on your TV rather than leaving your couch to actually go to the beach," says Kennedy.

1 ounce aged Demerara rum
(preferably Hamilton 86)

1 ounce rye
(preferably Rittenhouse)

1 ounce lemon juice

1 ounce coconut cream
(page 156)

½ ounce apricot liqueur

¼ ounce passion fruit syrup
(page 159)

GARNISH **lemon wheel, mint sprig**

Combine all the ingredients in a cocktail shaker. Add 1 large ice cube and shake until it melts. Strain into a Collins glass and top with crushed ice. Garnish with a lemon wheel and a mint sprig.

# SOUTHPAW SWIZZLE

ABIGAIL GULLO, BEN PARIS, SEATTLE

Abigail Gullo created the Southpaw Swizzle while working in New Orleans, and the drink answers that city's particular need for refreshing coolers year-round. Martinique rum brings a green, grassy note, and manzanilla sherry adds a certain nuttiness to the mix, while lime, coconut water, and Jamaican rum act as a tropical triple threat.

---

1 ounce manzanilla sherry

1 ounce unaged Martinique rum

¾ ounce honey syrup (page 155)

¾ ounce lime juice

1½ ounces coconut water

¾ ounce aged Jamaican rum

---

GARNISH   toasted coconut chips, lime wheel

Combine the sherry, Martinique rum, honey syrup, lime juice, and coconut water in a tall swizzle glass. Add crushed ice and swizzle until the glass begins to frost. Top with the Jamaican rum, then garnish with toasted coconut chips and a lime wheel.

# AMARO DI COCCO

RYAN LOTZ, SHORE LEAVE, BOSTON

A mash-up of a Piña Colada and a Negroni, the Amaro di Cocco marries Campari and sweet vermouth with Jamaican rum, coconut cream, and pineapple juice.

| | |
|---|---|
| 1 ounce aged Jamaican rum | ½ ounce black rum |
| 1 ounce Campari | 1½ ounces coconut cream (page 156) |
| 1 ounce sweet vermouth (preferably Dolin Rouge) | 1½ ounces pineapple juice |

Combine all the ingredients in a cocktail shaker. Add 1 cup crushed ice and shake for about 5 seconds. Pour into a tiki mug.

# COCO NO COCO

EZRA STAR, DRINK, BOSTON

Embodying the true *Easy Tiki* spirit, this four-ingredient recipe was first cobbled together to pass muster when a commonly called-for tiki ingredient was not readily on hand. "This is a fun one we use quite often when we run out of coconut cream," says Ezra Star, general manager of Boston's pioneering menu-less cocktail bar, Drink, which hosts a monthly tiki night. Standard heavy cream pairs with orgeat, pineapple juice, and aged Demerara rum for a full-bodied yet wholly refreshing mixture.

---

1½ ounces aged Demerara rum (preferably El Dorado 12 year)

¾ ounce heavy cream

¾ ounce pineapple juice

¾ ounce orgeat (page 158)

---

GARNISH   freshly grated nutmeg, grated cinnamon, tonka bean (optional)

Combine all the ingredients in a cocktail shaker. Add ice and shake briefly to integrate, about 5 seconds. Strain into a tiki mug or an extra-tall Collins glass filled with crushed ice. Garnish with freshly grated nutmeg, grated cinnamon, and a tonka bean, if desired.

# GUNGA DIN

## ST. JOHN FRIZELL, FORT DEFIANCE, BROOKLYN

Named for the 1890 poem by Rudyard Kipling, St. John Frizell's Gunga Din appropriately calls for a brand of Scottish gin by the name of Old Raj and asks to be shaken with cardamom pods, a spice native to India. As with all great tiki drinks, the Gunga Din takes the drinker on a transcontinental journey just by means of the ingredients in the glass.

---

3 cardamom pods

¾ ounce simple syrup (page 159)

2 ounces London dry gin (preferably Old Raj 110)

1 ounce pineapple juice

¾ ounce lime juice

Tonic water (preferably Q tonic), to top

---

GARNISH   pineapple fronds

Combine the cardamom pods and simple syrup in a cocktail shaker and muddle until fragrant. Add the gin, pineapple juice, and lime juice. Add ice and shake until chilled, about 10 seconds. Fine strain (see "fine-mesh strainer", page 51) into a tiki mug filled with ice. Top with tonic water and stir gently to combine. Garnish with pineapple fronds.

# SAMURAI'S DOWNFALL

BRIAN EVANS, SUNDAY IN BROOKLYN, BROOKLYN

While acting as bar director for Sunday in Brooklyn, Brian Evans also helmed the drinks program for a recurring pop-up called Yaki Tiki, which married Japanese cuisine and tiki cocktails. In his Samurai's Downfall, Evans builds on a low-proof shochu base and blends green shiso leaves directly into the mixture for an ultra-fresh, bright, and floral cocktail.

---

1½ ounces shochu (preferably Mizu Saga Barley)

½ ounce peach liqueur (preferably Giffard crème de pêche de vigne)

1 ounce pineapple juice

½ ounce honey

¾ ounce lime juice

5 green shiso leaves

---

GARNISH  pineapple wedge, cocktail umbrella

Combine all the ingredients in a blender. Add ¾ cup crushed ice and blend on low for 3 seconds. Increase the speed to high and blend for about 8 seconds, until the cocktail appears bright green. Pour into a hurricane glass. Garnish with a pineapple wedge and a cocktail umbrella.

# SPECTACLE ISLAND

CHANTAL TSENG, PETWORTH CITIZEN & READING ROOM,
WASHINGTON, DC

"In my fantasies, I wanted to encircle Spectacle Island
with a blazing corona of yellow flames, a beacon to ships
at sea, a landmark for airline pilots, permanent fireworks
for the yuppies in the new waterfront condos," writes Neal
Stephenson in his 1988 novel *Zodiac*. This passage served
as the inspiration for one of Chantal Tseng's many literary-
inspired cocktails. But while the island in question refers to
a Boston Harbor landmark, the drink recalls more distant
lands with Martinique rum, Portuguese Madeira, French
Chartreuse, and a tropical touch by way of pineapple.

---

¾ ounce unaged Martinique
rum (preferably Neisson Rhum
Agricole Blanc)

¾ ounce aged domestic
rum (preferably Thomas
Tew dark rum)

½ ounce lime juice

½ ounce pineapple juice

½ ounce Madeira (preferably
Saveiro "Vento do Oeste")

½ ounce green Chartreuse

---

GARNISH   mint sprig, lime shell soaked in overproof rum
(optional), freshly grated nutmeg

Combine all the ingredients in a tiki mug. Add crushed
ice until the mug is full and swizzle with a swizzle stick or
barspoon. Add more crushed ice to top the mug. Garnish
with a mint sprig, upside-down rum-soaked lime shell (if
using), and freshly grated nutmeg. Set the lime shell aflame
with a long match or kitchen lighter just before serving.

# CARROT COLADA

CHRISTINE WISEMAN, BROKEN SHAKER, LOS ANGELES

"This has kind of become my signature," says Christine Wiseman. "I love Piña Coladas more than any cocktail in the whole world." Though firmly in the colada family, the drink's inclusion of fresh carrot juice is Wiseman's nod to LA's obsession with fresh-pressed juices, and elements of spice, like pink peppercorn syrup, balance out the sweetness of the coconut cream and the tartness of the lemon juice. With its notes of clove, dried oranges, and coriander seeds, a measure of Amaro Montenegro adds even greater depth.

1½ ounces London dry gin

½ ounce Amaro Montenegro

½ ounce lemon juice

½ ounce marjoram and pink peppercorn syrup (page 159)

¾ ounce carrot juice

¾ ounce coconut cream (page 156)

GARNISH   carrot ribbons, edible flowers

Combine all the ingredients in a cocktail shaker. Add 1 large ice cube and shake until it melts. Pour into a tiki mug or hurricane glass. Add crushed ice to fill the glass and garnish with carrot ribbons and edible flowers.

# APRÈS-SKI SWIZZLE

NATHAN HAZARD, THE COCONUT CLUB, LOS ANGELES

Nathan Hazard's Après-Ski Swizzle reads like tiki on vacation in the Alps. The familiar tropical flavors are all there—rum, orgeat, pineapple, lime—joined by the 130 botanicals that make up Chartreuse's signature profile. The result is both tropical and herbaceous within a single sip.

---

1½ ounces lightly aged Barbados rum (preferably The Real McCoy 3 year)

1 ounce pineapple juice

¾ ounce green Chartreuse

½ ounce lime juice

½ ounce orgeat (page 158)

---

GARNISH   pineapple wedge, pineapple fronds, confectioners' sugar

Combine all the ingredients in a Zombie glass or tiki mug and top with crushed ice until full. Swizzle with a swizzle stick or barspoon until chilled, about 10 seconds. Add more crushed ice to fill the glass, if needed. Garnish with a pineapple wedge, pineapple fronds, and a dusting of confectioners' sugar.

# TEQUI LA BANANE

ORLANDO FRANKLIN MCCRAY, NIGHTMOVES, NEW YORK

To achieve robust fruit flavor without fresh fruit, Orlando Franklin McCray initially experimented with "fruit washing" this cocktail by infusing the base spirit with dehydrated passion fruit and banana powders. In this simplified rendition, however, he leans on fruit liqueurs in their place, while the inclusion of orgeat tilts this recipe firmly into tiki territory.

---

1½ ounces tequila (preferably La Gritona reposado)

½ ounce lemon juice

½ ounce orgeat (page 158)

¼ ounce banana liqueur (preferably Giffard Banane du Brésil)

¼ ounce passion fruit liqueur (preferably Giffard crème de fruit de la passion)

---

GARNISH  **Shaved almonds**

Combine all the ingredients in a cocktail shaker. Add a small scoop of crushed ice and shake until the ice has dissolved. Pour into a julep tin and fill the tin with cracked or crushed ice. Garnish with shaved almonds.

# A COY DECOY

CHRIS COY, THE INFERNO ROOM, INDIANAPOLIS

As offerings in the American gin category expand by the day, the botanical profile of the spirit has branched out well beyond the juniper-forward expressions typical of the London dry style. Here, Chris Coy deploys cucumber-heavy Uncle Val's gin alongside a more traditional expression from Fords, blending the two in a manner akin to how Don the Beachcomber married different styles of rum within a single drink. Combined with grapefruit liqueur and pineapple and lime juices, the Coy Decoy is bright, refreshing, and uniquely modern.

---

1 ounce London dry gin (preferably Fords)

½ ounce cucumber-forward gin (preferably Uncle Val's)

¾ ounce grapefruit liqueur (preferably Giffard crème de pamplemousse rose)

¾ ounce pineapple juice

¾ ounce lime juice

4 drops Bittermens Boston Bittahs

---

GARNISH    mint sprig, edible orchid, lime wheel

Combine all the ingredients in a cocktail shaker. Add ice and shake vigorously, about 30 seconds. Pour into a Zombie glass and garnish with mint, an edible orchid, and a lime wheel.

VARIATION    Combine all the ingredients in a drink mixer with 1 cup crushed ice. Buzz for 3 seconds. Pour into a Zombie glass, top with crushed ice, and garnish as directed.

# BITTER MAI TAI

JEREMY OERTEL, BROOKLYN

Perhaps the most riffed-upon cocktail in the tiki canon, the Mai Tai serves as the inspiration for Jeremy Oertel's decidedly bitter spin. Intrigued by a version he encountered that used Angostura bitters in place of rum, Oertel takes his bitter iteration in a different direction, incorporating red-hued Campari. A measure of funky Jamaican rum provides extra fortification in this version that has become a staple of Brooklyn bar Dram, where Oertel first created it.

1½ ounces Campari

¾ ounce aged Jamaican rum (preferably Smith & Cross)

½ ounce orange curaçao

¾ ounce orgeat (page 158)

1 ounce lime juice

GARNISH    mint bouquet

Combine all the ingredients in a cocktail shaker. Add ice and shake until chilled, about 10 seconds. Strain into a large rocks glass over crushed ice and garnish with a mint bouquet.

# MAI SHA ROA NA

ANTHONY SCHMIDT, FALSE IDOL, SAN DIEGO

At San Diego's False Idol, head bartender Anthony Schmidt looks to the Mai Tai as a continual source of inspiration for original cocktails. "The drink can be a fun lesson on building recipes," he says. "An infinite number of liqueurs can be swapped for the curaçao, leading to very different results." His Mai Sha Roa Na leans on banana liqueur in place of the orange liqueur, and macadamia nut syrup stands in for orgeat.

---

2 ounces aged overproof Jamaican rum

½ ounce banana liqueur (preferably Giffard Banane du Brésil or Tempus Fugit crème de banane)

½ ounce Orgeat Works Ltd macadamia nut syrup

¾ ounce lime juice

---

GARNISH   lime hull, mint sprig, dried banana chips (optional)

Combine all the ingredients in a cocktail shaker. Add 1½ cups cracked or crushed ice and shake briefly, two or three shakes. Pour into a double rocks glass. Garnish with a lime hull, a mint sprig, and some banana chips, if desired.

# KENTUCKY MAI TAI

DAN SABO, PALI SOCIETY, LOS ANGELES

The name of this Mai Tai riff nods to the source of its bourbon base, but that's not the only update Dan Sabo makes to the original. Mezcal, peach liqueur, and Cynar (a bittersweet Italian artichoke liqueur) make an appearance alongside the expected lemon and orgeat.

1 ounce bourbon (preferably Evan Williams Black Label)

1 ounce mezcal (preferably Nuestra Soledad Espadin Joven)

½ ounce Cynar

½ ounce peach liqueur (preferably Combier or Giffard crème de pêche de vigne)

½ ounce lemon juice

½ ounce orgeat (page 158, or Giffard)

GARNISH   mint sprig, cherry, pineapple slice

Combine all the ingredients in a cocktail shaker. Add ice and shake until chilled, about 10 seconds. Strain into a rocks glass half filled with crushed ice. Add more crushed ice to fill the glass. Garnish with a mint sprig, a cherry, and a pineapple slice.

# BREAKFAST MAI TAI

FANNY CHU, DONNA, BROOKLYN

The Breakfast Mai Tai has gone through several iterations at Donna, where it was first created with an oat orgeat for a guest who had a nut allergy. The recipe has evolved over the course of several menus, but its crushability remains intact. As Fanny Chu, the drink's creator, says, "I definitely would drink this for breakfast when vacationing somewhere tropical, or even on a day off, daydreaming of being in the tropics."

1½ ounces overproof Jamaican rum (preferably Smith & Cross)

½ ounce banana liqueur (preferably Giffard Banane du Brésil)

½ ounce orgeat (page 158)

¼ ounce cinnamon syrup (page 156)

1 ounce lime juice

¾ ounce black rum (preferably Hamilton)

GARNISH   mint sprig, charred cinnamon stick (see Note), edible flowers

Combine the overproof rum, banana liqueur, orgeat, cinnamon syrup, and lime juice in a cocktail shaker. Add a few pellets of crushed or cracked ice and shake until they melt. Pour into a large rocks glass, add the black rum, and top with more crushed ice. Garnish with a mint sprig, a charred cinnamon stick, and edible flowers.

NOTE   See page 46 for instructions on charring cinnamon sticks.

# CARIBE DAIQUIRI

PABLO MOIX, DAMA, LOS ANGELES

In his Caribe Daiquiri, Pablo Moix gives the age-old template an even more tropical spin with the inclusion of pineapple juice in addition to lime. True to the original construction of the Daiquiri, Moix uses dry sugar in place of simple syrup, making the recipe even easier to cobble together when the mood strikes.

---

**2 ounces unaged Puerto Rican rum (preferably Ron del Barrilito 2 Star)**

**¾ ounce pineapple juice**

**½ ounce lime juice**

**1 barspoon superfine sugar**

---

GARNISH **lime wedge**

Combine all the ingredients in a cocktail shaker. Add ice and shake until chilled, about 10 seconds. Strain into a coupe or cocktail glass and garnish with a lime wedge.

# CIRCE

CHANNING CENTENO, OTIS, BROOKLYN

Channing Centeno's Circe is spicy, rich, and bright all at once. Built on Batavia arrack, a funky molasses-and-rice-based distillate that predates rum, the mixture offers nuttiness courtesy of manzanilla sherry, floral notes from elderflower liqueur, and a double dose of spice from the combination of arrack and ginger syrup.

---

1 ounce Batavia Arrack van Oosten

½ ounce aged overproof Jamaican rum (preferably Plantation O.F.T.D)

¾ ounce manzanilla sherry

½ ounce St-Germain elderflower liqueur

¼ ounce ginger syrup (page 156)

¾ ounce lemon juice

---

GARNISH   3 grapes on a skewer

Combine all the ingredients in a cocktail shaker. Add ice and shake until chilled, about 10 seconds. Strain into a rocks glass over a large ice cube. Garnish with 3 grapes on a skewer.

# TROPIC OF CAPRICORN

LAUREN CORRIVEAU, NITECAP, NEW YORK

"Because Banana Daiquiris" is all Lauren Corriveau says about the inspiration behind her Tropic of Capricorn, a delicate, herbaceous spin on (you guessed it) a Banana Daiquiri. Green tea–infused rum adds a subtle grassy note to the requisite lime juice and banana liqueur, while a teaspoon of fernet amplifies the herbal qualities and provides a cooling finish.

---

2 ounces green tea–infused Demerara rum (page 158)

¼ ounce banana liqueur (preferably Tempus Fugit crème de banane)

¾ ounce lime juice

½ ounce cane syrup (see simple syrup variation, page 159)

1 teaspoon Fernet-Branca

---

Combine all the ingredients in a cocktail shaker. Add ice and shake until chilled, about 10 seconds. Strain into a coupe or cocktail glass.

# JAMAICAN MULE

JELANI JOHNSON, CLOVER CLUB, BROOKLYN

With a particular interest in house-made syrups and infusions, it's not uncommon for Jelani Johnson's original tiki drinks to incorporate elaborate components, like *quatre épices* syrup, inspired by the four-spice blend often called for in French cooking, or a coconut-orgeat blend. Here he takes a decidedly more straightforward approach, calling on what he dubs his "favorite tried-and-true flavor combo." Building off a base of Jamaican rum, he adds the ginger and lime components of a classic mule, along with a good dose of fresh pineapple juice and a finishing touch of Angostura bitters.

---

2 ounces aged Jamaican rum (preferably Appleton Estate V/X)

1 ounce ginger syrup (page 156)

¾ ounce lime juice

½ ounce pineapple juice

2 dashes Angostura bitters

---

GARNISH   candied ginger slice on a pick, lime wheel, edible orchid

Combine all the ingredients in a cocktail shaker. Add ½ cup crushed ice and shake for about 5 seconds. Pour into a Pilsner glass filled with crushed ice. Garnish with candied ginger on a pick, a lime wheel, and an edible orchid.

# MAKALAPA

LYNNETTE MARRERO, LLAMA INN, BROOKLYN

Translated from the Hawaiian for "rigid features," the Makalapa shares its name with a neighborhood in Honolulu situated on a crater lake. The drink itself, however, makes a softer impression. In a nod to Hawaii's state flower, Lynnette Marrero calls on a simple hibiscus honey syrup to add body to the mixture of blended aged rum and two types of citrus. To finish, she adds a topper of soda water for subtle effervescence.

---

**2 ounces blended aged rum or Demerara rum**

**½ ounce lime juice**

**½ ounce grapefruit juice**

**1 ounce hibiscus honey syrup (page 155)**

**½ ounce soda water**

---

Combine the rum, lime juice, grapefruit juice, and hibiscus honey syrup in a cocktail shaker. Add ice and shake until chilled, about 10 seconds. Strain into a coupe. Top with the soda water.

# SLEEPING LOTUS

SIERRA KIRK, HALE PELE, PORTLAND, OREGON

The Sleeping Lotus drinks like the Army & Navy cocktail on leave in the Bahamas. Rather than being served in a buttoned-up fashion, in a coupe with no garnish, the Sleeping Lotus relaxes over crushed ice in a Zombie glass, topped with an edible orchid and copious mint. To the expected gin, orgeat, and lemon, mint adds a cooling element, while orange bitters add a bitter citrus note.

---

2 ounces dry gin

1 ounce orgeat (page 158)

¾ ounce lemon juice

2 dashes orange bitters

10 mint leaves

---

GARNISH   **edible orchid, mint sprig**

Combine all the ingredients in a cocktail shaker. Add ice and shake until chilled, about 10 seconds. Strain into a Zombie or Collins glass filled with crushed ice and stir to incorporate. Top with more crushed ice. Garnish with an edible orchid and a mint sprig.

# JAH RULE

JESSICA MANZEY, SEATTLE

In addition to funky aged Jamaican rum, Jessica Manzey's Jah Rule looks to cachaça, South America's sugarcane spirit. Together, the two offer a bold banana and tropical base note, which is complemented by the bitter, herbal qualities of Luxardo Bitter Bianco and the zestiness of lime.

---

1 ounce cachaça (preferably Novo Fogo Silver)

1 ounce aged Jamaican rum (preferably Doctor Bird)

½ ounce Luxardo Bitter Bianco

½ ounce lime juice

1 dash absinthe

---

Combine all the ingredients in a cocktail shaker. Add ice and shake until chilled, about 10 seconds. Strain into a tiki mug or rocks glass filled with crushed ice.

# ISLAND TO ISLAY PUNCH

TAYLOR RAE ADORNO, GHOST DONKEY, NEW YORK

In this twist on a Bajan rum punch, Taylor Rae Adorno adds a hint of smoke by way of peated Scotch atop a rum base. Passion fruit and lime add a sweet-tart kick, while cinnamon brings the requisite spice. "Yummy and simple," says Adorno of her update to the timeless punch template.

---

2 ounces aged Barbados rum (preferably Mount Gay Eclipse)

½ ounce peated Scotch (preferably Bruichladdich Port Charlotte)

1 ounce passion fruit juice

½ ounce cinnamon syrup (page 156)

¾ ounce lime juice

2 dashes Bittermens 'Elemakule Tiki Bitters

---

GARNISH   freshly grated nutmeg

Combine all the ingredients in a cocktail shaker. Add ice and shake until chilled, about 10 seconds. Pour into a Collins glass and garnish with freshly grated nutmeg.

# AUSTRAL SUMMER

ERYN REECE, BANZARBAR, NEW YORK

"This drink is a blend of two of my favorite classic cocktails," says New York bartender Eryn Reece, "the Champs Elysees and Cameron's Kick—with a touch of coconut." Blending the brandy and green Chartreuse components of the former with the Irish whiskey of the latter and adding a splash of coconut liqueur, Reece lands on a hybrid concoction that is, in her words, "the best of both worlds."

---

1½ ounces brandy (preferably Monteru)

½ ounce Irish whiskey (preferably Redbreast 12 year)

¾ ounce lemon juice

½ ounce coconut liqueur (preferably Kalani coconut rum liqueur)

½ ounce green Chartreuse

1 dash Angostura bitters

---

GARNISH   banana leaf

Combine all the ingredients in a cocktail shaker with a few pellets of crushed or cracked ice and shake until they melt. Pour into a Collins glass and fill the glass with crushed ice. Garnish with a banana leaf.

# GOOD ENOUGH GATSBY

SEAN QUINN, DEATH & CO., DENVER

In the style of Trader Vic, Sean Quinn demonstrates whiskey's ability to be just as much of a summer go-to as it is a winter standby. The spiciness of rye is backed up by cinnamon syrup, while unaged pear eau de vie and pineapple juice bring a brightness that keeps the drink in balance. To round out the cocktail, Quinn calls on a teaspoon of Fernet-Branca for a bracing, cooling flourish.

---

1½ ounces rye
(preferably Wild Turkey 101)

½ ounce pear eau de vie
(preferably Clear Creek)

¾ ounce cinnamon syrup
(page 156)

¾ ounce pineapple juice

½ ounce lime juice

1 teaspoon Fernet-Branca

---

GARNISH   **pineapple fronds, grated cinnamon**

Combine all the ingredients in a cocktail shaker. Add ice and shake until chilled, about 10 seconds. Strain into a large rocks glass filled with crushed ice. Garnish with pineapple fronds and grated cinnamon.

# MORALE & WELFARE

RYAN LOTZ, SHORE LEAVE, BOSTON

"This is essentially a short version of the classic Jet Pilot, served up," explains bartender Ryan Lotz, referencing the 1958 recipe created by Stephen Crane at his famous Luau Restaurant in Beverly Hills. By using one rum instead of three and omitting absinthe and falernum, Lotz manages to create a simplified version that still channels the spirit and complexity of the original, albeit on a shorter plan.

---

1½ ounces aged overproof rum (preferably Plantation O.F.T.D.)

¾ ounce cinnamon syrup (page 156)

¾ ounce lime juice

½ ounce grapefruit juice

2 dashes mole bitters

---

Combine all the ingredients in a cocktail shaker. Add ice and shake until chilled, about 10 seconds. Strain into a coupe.

# SYRUPS

## GARDENIA MIX

MAKES   **about 1½ cups**

**½ pound butter**
**½ quart honey**
**⅛ cup boiling water**

**½ ounce vanilla extract**
**1 teaspoon Maldon smoked salt**
**¼ cup Trader Vic's macadamia nut liqueur (optional)**

In a saucepan, heat the butter over medium-high heat. Once the butter starts to foam, after about 5 minutes, stir it with a spatula, making sure that the butter browns without burning. Once it takes on a toffee color, remove the pan from the heat and let cool.

In a blender, combine the honey and boiling water and blend until integrated. Add the lukewarm brown butter, vanilla, salt, and macadamia nut liqueur (if using). Blend on high speed until well combined. Pour into a lidded container and store in the refrigerator until ready to use. (If chilled, the mixture may need to loosen up in a heatproof container set in boiling water prior to using.)

## HIBISCUS HONEY SYRUP

MAKES   **about 1 cup**

**½ cup hot hibiscus tea**          **½ cup honey**

In a small tempered container, combine the hot tea and honey and stir until incorporated. Store in the refrigerator for up to 2 weeks.

## HONEY SYRUP

MAKES   **about 2 cups**

**1 cup honey**          **1 cup water**

In a small saucepan, combine the honey and water over low heat, stirring, until fully incorporated. Remove from the heat and let cool. Store in an airtight container in the refrigerator for up to 2 weeks.

# CINNAMON SYRUP

MAKES   about 1½ cups

½ ounce (16 grams)
Saigon cinnamon bark,
broken into pieces

1 cup sugar

1 cup water

In a small saucepan, briefly toast the cinnamon over medium heat until fragrant, 3 to 5 minutes. Add the sugar and water and bring to just under a boil, stirring until the sugar has dissolved. Remove from the heat and let cool. Strain into an airtight container and store at room temperature for up to 24 hours or in the refrigerator for up to 2 weeks.

# COCONUT CREAM

MAKES   about 2 cups

1 cup canned full-fat
coconut milk

1 cup cream of coconut

In a medium bowl, whisk together the coconut milk and cream of coconut until incorporated. Store in an airtight container in the refrigerator for up to 2 weeks.

# GINGER SYRUP

MAKES   about 1¾ cups

1½ cups sugar

1½ cups water

1 cup ginger juice

In a medium saucepan, combine the sugar and water over medium heat, stirring until the sugar has dissolved. Remove from the heat, add the ginger juice, and stir until fully incorporated. Let cool, then store in an airtight container in the refrigerator for up to 2 weeks.

NOTE   If you don't have a juicer, look for fresh pressed ginger juice at health food stores or juiceries.

## DONN'S MIX

MAKES **about 3 cups**

**1 cup cinnamon syrup**
**(facing page)**

**2 cups grapefruit juice**
**(from about 2 grapefruits)**

In a medium jar or other container with a lid, stir together the cinnamon syrup and grapefruit juice until well combined. Cover and store in the refrigerator for up to 1 week.

## DONN'S SPICES #2

MAKES **about 3 cups**

**2 cups sugar**

**2 cups water**

**1 teaspoon vanilla bean paste**

**¾ ounce pimento dram**
**(preferably St. Elizabeth)**

In a medium saucepan, combine the sugar, water, and vanilla over medium heat, stirring until the sugar has dissolved, about 5 minutes. Remove from the heat, add the pimento dram, and stir until fully combined. Let cool, then transfer to an airtight container and store in the refrigerator for up to 2 weeks.

## GRENADINE

MAKES **about 1½ cups**

**1 cup unsweetened**
**pomegranate juice**

**1 cup sugar**

In a small saucepan, heat ½ cup of the pomegranate juice over medium-low heat until it has reduced to a quarter of its original volume (about 2 tablespoons). Add the remaining ½ cup pomegranate juice and the sugar and stir until the sugar has dissolved. Let cool, then store in an airtight container in the refrigerator for up to 2 weeks. (See store-bought options, page 44.)

# GREEN TEA–INFUSED DEMERARA RUM

MAKES **750 ml**

**5 grams loose leaf green tea**   **1 (750 ml) bottle Demerara rum**

Add the green tea to the bottle of rum and let sit for 30 minutes. Strain off the tea leaves and rebottle. Store at room temperature indefinitely.

# ORGEAT

MAKES **about 2 cups**

**½ pound (300 grams)**   **Water, as needed**
**raw almonds**
                          **Sugar, as needed**

Put the almonds in a bowl and add water to cover. Set aside to soak overnight. Drain the water, then weigh the almonds. Transfer them to a blender and slowly add an equal weight of fresh water while the blender is running on low speed for about 1 minute. Increase to high speed and blend until the mixture is opaque. Strain through a fine-mesh strainer lined with cheesecloth. Weigh the strained milk. Transfer to a saucepan and add an equal weight of sugar. Over medium heat, stir until the sugar has dissolved. Remove from the heat and let cool. Store in an airtight container in the refrigerator for up to 2 weeks. (See store-bought options, page 44.)

# RICH DEMERARA SYRUP

MAKES **about 2 cups**

**2 cups Demerara sugar**   **1 cup water**

In a medium saucepan, combine the sugar and water over medium-low heat, stirring until the sugar has dissolved. Remove from the heat and let cool. Store in an airtight container in the refrigerator for up to 2 weeks.

## MARJORAM AND PINK PEPPERCORN SYRUP

MAKES   **about 2 cups**

2 cups simple syrup (below)

1 tablespoon fresh
marjoram leaves

1 tablespoon whole
pink peppercorns

In a blender, combine all the ingredients and blend until smooth. Strain through a fine-mesh sieve and discard the solids. Store in an airtight container in the refrigerator for up to 2 weeks.

## PASSION FRUIT SYRUP

MAKES   **about 2 cups**

1¼ cups water

1¼ cups sugar

¼ cup thawed frozen passion
fruit concentrate (preferably
The Perfect Purée of Napa
Valley or Ravlfruit)

In a saucepan, combine the water and sugar over medium-low heat, stirring until the sugar has dissolved. Transfer to a medium container and stir in the passion fruit until incorporated into the syrup. Cover and store in the refrigerator for up to 2 weeks.

## SIMPLE SYRUP

MAKES   **about 1½ cups**

1 cup sugar

1 cup water

In a small saucepan, combine the sugar and water over medium-low heat, stirring until the sugar has dissolved. Remove from the heat and let cool. Store in an airtight container in the refrigerator for up to 2 weeks.

**VARIATION**   Cane sugar can be used in place of granulated sugar for a more richly flavored cane syrup.

# Appendix: Where to Tiki

Tiki has become so pervasive that it's breached the walls of its namesake bars and now appears on menus at even the most buttoned-up cocktail spots. But following are the institutions, both historic and modern, that hold true to the all-encompassing aspect of tiki—décor, music, and philosophy included. In other words, this is where to find tiki in all its extravagant glory.

## Historic

### HALA KAHIKI (RIVER GROVE, ILLINOIS)
One of the Midwest's oldest remaining tiki bars, Hala Kahiki declares on their website, "We were tiki before it was cool." A River Grove, Illinois, standby since 1952 (and at its current location since 1964), the bar is a testament to the far reaches of tiki during its midcentury heyday, when even locations as un-tiki as Columbus and Chicago came down with tropical fever.

### KAHALA (BARCELONA, SPAIN)
While Barcelona was once home to more than a dozen tiki bars, Kahala is one of the few remaining from the country's 1970s tiki tryst. Though it dates from just outside the golden age of tiki, Spain's first tiki bar still boasts all the classic trappings: a waterfall entrance, volcanic stone sculptures, bamboo booths, and a fish pond replete with piranhas.

### MAI-KAI (FORT LAUDERDALE, FLORIDA)
When Jack and Bob Thornton opened the Mai-Kai in Fort Lauderdale in 1956, it was the most expensive restaurant ever built. The Polynesiac brothers outfitted their joint venture with décor amassed on a two-month journey to the South Pacific; the pair returned with twenty-three tons of artifacts and souvenirs that would go on to line their soaring A-frame space, which also housed a 30,000-square-foot tropical garden. Today, the Mai-Kai remains a family-run business, still serving their famous Mystery Drink accompanied by a gong ceremonially rung by the Mai-Kai Mystery Girl.

### TIKI-TI (LOS ANGELES, CALIFORNIA)
This postage-stamp-size bar can still be found perched in its original location on Sunset Boulevard. Opened in 1961 by Ray Buhen, a former Don the Beachcomber bartender, today the twelve-seat bar is operated by Buhen's son and grandsons. With ninety-four signature cocktails, including the famed Ooga-Booga (when ordered everybody chants "ooga-booga"), the Tiki-Ti is perhaps more kitsch than craft, but it's also the ultimate tiki time warp.

### TONGA ROOM & HURRICANE BAR (SAN FRANCISCO, CALIFORNIA)

Located in the basement of the Fairmont San Francisco hotel, the Tonga Room has been serving guests since 1945. The centerpiece of the historic bar is the "lagoon," a plunge pool redesigned by Hollywood set director Mel Melvin, with a thatch-roofed barge on which bands perform throughout the evening. Intermittently, a tropical rain shower is re-created over the pool.

### TRAD'R SAM (SAN FRANCISCO, CALIFORNIA)

Though much of the bamboo-laden décor has remained unchanged since its 1937 opening, time has done a number on Trad'r Sam. Today, the Trad'r is decidedly lowbrow—bananas do not hang from the back bar and the bartenders no longer wear pit helmets, but it still promises the carefree atmosphere of any good dive, with a few tropical flourishes.

### TRADER VIC'S (ATLANTA, GEORGIA)

Of all the Trader Vic's locations in the US, the property in Atlanta is the only one that has not suffered any loss to its original interior décor. Opened in 1976, it remains a time capsule of tiki's imaginary exoticism—faux African masks hang alongside Japanese fishing buoys in a bamboo-clad interior.

### TRADER VIC'S (LONDON, UNITED KINGDOM)

Opened in 1963 in the basement of the Hilton on Park Lane, the Trader Vic's in London represents the first international outpost for the franchise. As numerous locations have been shuttered over the years, it's also become the oldest operating outpost of the chain. Though it was remodeled in 2014 following a fire in the hotel, the bar and restaurant still retain much of the original interior, and cocktails are served in signature Trader Vic drinkware.

### TRADER VIC'S (MUNICH, GERMANY)

Opened in 1971 in Hotel Bayerischer Hof, the Munich location is the second-oldest still-operating Trader Vic's. Though the bar launched when tiki was on the decline, the decked-out interior, with oversize wood carvings and a thatched ceiling, recalls the ambience of golden-age tiki bars.

### TRADER VIC'S (TOKYO, JAPAN)

The Tokyo Trader Vic's is a particularly notable specimen for tikiphiles in part because it is the only location still serving Vic Bergeron's original recipes (as opposed to drinks created at Trader Vic's but not by the man himself). Located on the fourth floor of the Garden Tower in the Hotel New Otani, the bar opened in 1974 and remains popular with a high-end clientele who come for the cigars and cocktails served in rare, original drinkware.

## Modern

**BEACHBUM BERRY'S LATITUDE 29 (NEW ORLEANS, LOUISIANA)**
Opened in 2014 by tiki historian, author, collector, and bartender Jeff "Beachbum" Berry, Latitude 29 offers a space where the Don the Beachcomber code cracker can finally serve the drinks he saved from the brink of extinction.

**THE BEACHCOMBER (LONDON, UNITED KINGDOM)**
The Beachcomber opened its doors in West London in 2013 and boasts one of the largest collections of rhum agricole outside the Caribbean, which, along with its bamboo bar, rattan lamps, and tropical décor, draws a nightly crowd of local tikiphiles.

**BOOTLEGGER TIKI (PALM SPRINGS, CALIFORNIA)**
Located in the former Don the Beachcomber space on Palm Canyon Drive in Palm Springs, California, Bootlegger Tiki aims to preserve the town's tiki tradition with a mix of original and classic tiki cocktails.

**DIRTY DICK (PARIS, FRANCE)**
Originally from Southern California, Dirty Dick owner Scotty Schuder converted this former brothel into a world-class tiki bar in 2013. The menu respects the tiki classics, and one of the bar's most popular cocktails is his Missionary's Downfall (page 64), a frozen pineapple-and-mint-inflected Daiquiri.

**FALSE IDOL (SAN DIEGO, CALIFORNIA)**
Hidden behind San Diego's Craft & Commerce cocktail bar is False Idol, where the cocktail list was developed by Martin Cate and beverage director Anthony Schmidt, two key figures in the modern revival, with over-the-top décor by Bamboo Ben.

**FOUNDATION BAR (MILWAUKEE, WISCONSIN)**
Milwaukee's premier tiki den, Foundation Bar opened as a punk bar in 1995 but by 2004 had morphed into the immersive tiki bar it is today. Since 2017, the space above the bar has been converted into a tiki-themed hotel known as the Captain's Quarters.

**HALE PELE (PORTLAND, OREGON)**
In a slightly suburban quarter of Portland, Hale Pele, with its large-scale tiki carvings and simulated rainfall on the roof, acts as a portal to another world.

### THE INFERNO ROOM (INDIANAPOLIS, INDIANA)

The newly opened Inferno Room is doing its part to bring tiki back to the Midwest by committing its menu to Don the Beachcomber, Trader Vic, and Steve Crane recipes, alongside a selection of house-made drinks from their own "infernal tribe." Of note are the many artifacts that adorn the walls, believed to be the largest collection of native Papua New Guinea art outside a museum.

### LAST RITES (SAN FRANCISCO, CALIFORNIA)

Part of a growing movement of "Polynesian Noir" bars that lean in to the darker, more melancholy underbelly of tiki, the bar at Last Rites is built to look like the fuselage of a crashed airplane, while six-foot-tall skulls loom over booths in this goth-inspired tiki bar.

### LEI LOW (HOUSTON, TEXAS)

At Lei Low, Houston's response to the tiki revival sweeping much of the country, it's not uncommon to see Southeast Texas spins on classic tiki formulas.

### LOST LAKE (CHICAGO, ILLINOIS)

Logan Square's Lost Lake, with its banana-leaf wallpaper and top-tier rum collection, is a worthy successor to Chicago's bygone tiki bars.

### MAX'S SOUTH SEAS HIDEAWAY (GRAND RAPIDS, MICHIGAN)

Opened in October 2019, Max's South Seas Hideaway is a three-story tiki oasis located in a historic property in downtown Grand Rapids. The first tiki bar of this scale to open in the twenty-first century, Max's South Seas Hideaway represents the combined efforts of several of the tiki world's most distinguished figures, including Martin Cate, Mark Sellers, and Gecko.

### MUTINY BAR (DETROIT, MICHIGAN)

Detroit's sole tiki bar, Mutiny, which opened in 2017, is equal parts kitschy and classic. The space retains much of its former appearance as a dive bar, but bamboo additions and glass fishing floats hint at the tiki theme, which is on clear display in the drinks served.

## PACIFIC SEAS AT CLIFTON'S (LOS ANGELES, CALIFORNIA)
Though the original iteration of Clifton's opened two years before Don the Beachcomber's on North McCadden Place, the bar that stands in its place today has much in common with the tiki greats, particularly in its vision for a mythical South Seas atmosphere.

## PAGAN IDOL (SAN FRANCISCO, CALIFORNIA)
Much like the tiki temples of yore, Pagan Idol goes all in on the tiki aesthetic, with two interior rooms offering distinct moods—one nautical, with portholes depicting maritime scenes; one tropical, with thatched huts. An erupting volcano is the cherry on top.

## PORCO LOUNGE & TIKI ROOM (CLEVELAND, OHIO)
Until Porco Lounge & Tiki Room opened in 2013, Cleveland had been tiki-less since the closing of the famed Kon-Tiki in 1976. Some of the original décor from the Kon-Tiki, however, including lamps and bamboo details, has found its way into the interior of Porco Lounge & Tiki Room.

## SHORE LEAVE (BOSTON, MASSACHUSETTS)
Named for a sailor's time on dry land at various ports of call, Shore Leave is Boston's only dedicated tiki bar and is not to be missed.

## SMUGGLER'S COVE (SAN FRANCISCO, CALIFORNIA)
Smuggler's Cove is the award-winning cocktail bar from owner Martin Cate, who is responsible for the bar's much-lauded menu and unique rum club, the Rumbustion Society.

## TRADER SAM'S ENCHANTED TIKI BAR (ANAHEIM, CALIFORNIA)
Located at the Disneyland Hotel in Anaheim, California, Trader Sam's Enchanted Tiki Bar quickly became a destination when it opened in 2011 and remains so today.

## TRAILER HAPPINESS (LONDON, UNITED KINGDOM)
Tucked into London's Portobello Road, Trailer Happiness has been serving its eccentric take on tiki since 2003 without a lapse in quality.

## ZOMBIE VILLAGE (SAN FRANCISCO, CALIFORNIA)
The recently opened bar from the team behind Pagan Idol has a Trader Vic alum—Daniel "Doc" Parks—helming the cocktail program, while the interior features the work of tiki artists Bamboo Ben and Ivan Mora.

## Acknowledgments

Thanks first and foremost to Jeff "Beachbum" Berry, whose hard work
has made enjoying tiki easy for the rest of us. Thank you to my editors,
Talia Baiocchi, Ashley Pierce, and Kim Keller, for their guidance; to the
PUNCH and Ten Speed Press teams for their support; to Lizzie Munro
for being so good at her hobby; to Martin Cate for his time and insight;
to Paul McGee for answering my endless questions about rum; to all the
bartenders included in these pages for their enthusiasm, expertise, and
delicious recipes; with special thanks to Austin Hartman, Jane Danger,
Jelani Johnson, and Garret Richard; and to those keeping the tiki spirit
alive. *Mahalo nui loa.*

## About the Author

Chloe Frechette is the senior editor at PUNCH and regularly contributes
articles on tiki and cocktail culture. She has a master's degree in history
of design from the Royal College of Art, where she earned distinction for
her research on the material culture of cocktail consumption.

# Index

## A
Allison, Shelby, 37
Amaro di Cocco, 117
Après-Ski Swizzle, 126
Austral Summer, 148

## B
Baldwin's (Easy) Sherry Colada, 109
batching, 54–55
Beach, Donn (Don the Beachcomber;
    Ernest Gantt), 2, 3, 9, 10, 15,
    21–24, 26–27, 34, 37, 41–42, 44,
    45, 46, 50, 59, 60, 62, 64, 69,
    71, 72, 90, 98, 129
Bergeron, Vic (Trader Vic), 23, 26, 27,
    34, 42, 44, 45, 50, 60, 77, 79, 82,
    83, 84, 86, 88, 90, 104, 161
Berry, Jeff "Beachbum," 3–4, 9, 10, 11,
    15, 26, 31, 33, 34–35, 36, 61, 62,
    72, 88, 162
Bitter Mai Tai, 130
Breakfast Mai Tai, 135
Brownlee, Edward, 15
Buhen, Ray, 24, 160

## C
Caribe Daiquiri, 136
Carrot Colada, 124
Cate, Martin, 10, 11, 22, 31, 36, 74, 77,
    162, 163, 164
Cinnamon Syrup, 156
Circe, 138
Cobra's Fang, 68
Coco No Coco, 118
Coconut Cream, 44, 156
A Coy Decoy, 129

## D
daiquiris
    Caribe Daiquiri, 136
    Don's Special Daiquiri, 69
Demerara Dry Float, 67
Donga Punch, 61
Donn's Mix, 157
Donn's Spices #2, 157

Don's Beachcombers Café, 21–22,
    23, 24
Don's Special Daiquiri, 69
Don the Beachcomber (bar), 4, 9, 22,
    24, 31, 33, 34, 61
Don the Beachcomber (person).
    *See* Beach, Donn

## E
Eastern Sour, 88
Elusive Dreams, 98

## F
falernum, 35, 50
Fog Cutter, 79

## G
Gantt, Ernest Raymond Beaumont.
    *See* Beach, Donn
Gardenia Mix, 155
garnishes, 46
Ginger Syrup, 156
glassware, 12
Good Enough Gatsby, 151
Green Tea–Infused Demerara
    Rum, 158
Grenadine, 44, 157
Grog, Trader Vic's, 74
Gunga Din, 121

## H
Haigh, Ted, 35
Hibiscus Honey Syrup, 155
Hinky Dinks, 23, 27
Honey Syrup, 44, 155

## I
ice, 49, 54
Improved Bajan Rum Punch, 92
Iron Ranger, 104
Island to Islay Punch, 147

## J
Jah Rule, 146
Jamaican Mule, 141
Junior Colada, 97